Chris Flaherty

TURKISH ARMY & NAVY 1861-1876

SOLDIERS&WEAPONS 042

SOLDIERSHOP PUBLISHING

AUTHOR

Since 2009, Chris Flaherty has written for the UK Armourer Magazine; Classic Arms & Militaria; and, Soldier of the Queen Journal. He has advised major international museums on uniforms. For Partizan Press in 2014, he wrote and illustrated two books: 'Turkish Uniforms of the Crimean War: A Handbook of Uniforms'; and, 'The Ottoman Army in the First World War: A Handbook of Uniforms'. He co-authored and illustrated with Bruno Mugnai for Soldiershop Publishing: 2014 'Der Lange Turkenkrieg (1593-1606), Volume. 1: The Long Turkish – War Habsburg Arrests the Ottoman Advance; and, in 2015 'Der Lange Turkenkrieg (1593- 1606), Volume. 2: The Long Turkish War'. In 2015, he was a contributor (illustrator) to theTurkish Gallipoli Centenary Exhibition: 'From Depths to the Trenches: Gallipoli 1915', at the Isbank Museum in Istanbul. Chris Flaherty was one of the contributors to, 'Philip Jowett, 2015 Armies of the Greek-Turkish War 1919–22', Men-at-Arms 50, Osprey Publishing. He authored a chapter on the, 'Ottoman Army in the Great Northern War' appearing in Stephen, L. Kling, Jr. (Editor) 2016 GNW Compendium: A Collection of Articles on the Great Northern War, 1700-1721 (Volume: 2), The Historical Game Company.

Chris Flaherty has authored and illustrated for Partizan Press' Universal Wargames Rules Supplements: 'Napoleonic Small Siege, River Ship, Gunboat and Pontooning' (2016); 'Napoleonic Foraging, Insurrection, Marauders, Bakeries, Convoy and Encampment Wargaming' (2016); 'Napoleonic Balloon Warfare' (2017); 'Napoleonic Ottoman Army Wargaming Supplement' (2018); 'A Wargamer's Guide to WW1 Ottoman Army Uniforms' (2018); 'Napoleon's July 1798 Pyramid Campaign & the Egyptian Army' (2019); 'The Napoleonic Ottoman Army: Uniforms, Tactics and Organization' (2019). In 2021 he wrote and illustrated 'The Sardinian Expeditionary Corps' and 'Turkish Army Crimean War Uniforms' in two volumes for Soldiershop Publishing.

PUBLISHER'S NOTES

LICENSES COMMONS

ISBN: 978-88-93278690   1st edition June 2022
S&W-042 - TURKISH ARMY & NAVY 1861-1876
Written and illustrated by Chris Flaherty
Editor: Luca Cristini Editore, for the brand: Soldiershop. Cover & Art Design: Luca S. Cristini.

CONTENTS

Introduction..p.5

Chapter 1: Army Organization and Infantry..p.15

Chapter 2: Rank Insignia and Officer's Uniforms...p.25

Chapter 3: Personal Equipment and Muskets...p.33

Chapter 4: Sultan's Standard, Sanjakdar: Standard Bearer and Imam du Regiment.............p.37

Chapter 5: Gendarmery, Garde du Palais and Court Security Officers...................p.41

Chapter 6: Cavalry..p.43

Chapter 7: Artillery...p.55

Chapter 8: Albanians...p.59

Chapter 9: Bashi-Bazouks..p.63

Chapter 10: Navy...p.71

References..p.83

▲ Sultan Abdulaziz was the 32nd Sultan of the Ottoman Empire and reigned between 25 June 1861 and 30 May 1876. Pictured here, he wears an early pattern Army Officer's tunic, and brocade belt and standard upwards pointing crescent buckle. His special pointed cuffs displays an early Ottoman coat of arms, and end with a crescent badge (not visible in the photograph – but seen in many other versions of this same sitting)[1].

<hr>

1 Unknown, 1861.

INTRODUCTION

This book looks at the Turkish Army and Navy during the Era of Sultan Abdulaziz, the 32nd Sultan of the Ottoman Empire, who reigned between 25 June 1861 and 30 May 1876. Both the Army and Navy changed its appearance substantially, from the Crimean War Period. The most notable of the 1861 Era changes was adoption of a standardized system for rank identification than had existed previously. It was based on using an arrangement of gold or silver chevrons placed above the tunic cuff. The introduction of a Zouave uniform based on French Army versions were used by the bulk of the Turkish Army. The other major change to occur under Sultan Abdulaziz was a massive purchase campaign for new Infantry small arms, Artillery and ironclad warships modernization.

1861 SULTAN ABDULMECID ARMY AND NAVY UNIFORMS

The 1861 Era begins with the end of the reign for Sultan Abdulmecid who died on 25 June 1861. In the remaining years following the end of the Crimean War, the Turkish Army and Navy began to change its appearance. By 1861, standard dress for Officers, and Soldiers in the Army or Navy had become a looser fitting low collared, dark blue frock coat with a single line of buttons down the front[2]. Long coat skirts reached down to the knees. The Fez, with light blue trousers or breeches, and black shoes or riding boots completed the dress. A prototype-version of the Zouave uniform for the Infantry Soldier also appeared in the last year. Uniforms were much plainer than had been seen in the Crimean War Period, and had a strong resemblance to either French or United States uniforms worn in the same year. Several figures are known from a set of Court Uniform illustrations that possibly date to early-1861, and relate to the final year of Sultan Abdulmecid, and these show a Feriq [Ferik]: General de Division, Colonel d'Infantry: Infantry Colonel, Colonel d'Artillerie: Artillery Colonel, Capitaine: Captain, and Officer de Marine: Navy Officer.

The Infantry Colonel's uniform is a plain blue frock coat with no coloured tape decoration and low red collar. The cuffs are round and red, with a gold tape edge, and more gold floral embroidery. A red waist sash is worn under a brocade belt. Light blue trousers with gold side stripes and black shoes complete the dress.

The Artillery Colonel's uniform is a plain blue frock coat with no coloured tape decoration and low red collar. The red cuffs are pointed with a broad gold tape chevron over these. Gold shoulder cords are worn. A white carry strap is used for the Cavalry cartridge box. This has a crescent badge on it, and grenade badge below it. A red waist sash is worn. Light blue breaches with gold side stripes and black riding boots complete the dress.

The Infantry Captain's uniform is interesting as this depicts a plain blue frock coat with no coloured tape decoration and folded down low collar revealing possibly yellow lining (this was a United States practice for Officers to fold their collars down). The only decoration on the coat are gold epaulette bridles fitted to the shoulders. The coat is unbuttoned revealing a collarless plain blue waist coat, white shirt and low cravat-neck stock. A wide red waist sash is worn. Light blue breaches and black riding boots complete the dress.

The Navy Officer's uniform is a plain blue frock coat with no coloured tape decoration and low yellow collar that appears to have a blue tape edge. There are no epaulette bridles. A red waist sash is worn. Light blue trousers with gold side stripes and black shoes complete the dress.

A 1907 illustration shows a Sultan Abdulmecid Period figure identified as an Officer d'Artillerie: Artillery Officer, with cuff chevrons over pointed cuffs[3]. Similarly, the Feriq [Ferik]: General de Division, and Artillery Colonel both display cuff chevrons, suggesting the rank system was being introduced under Sultan Abdulmecid by 1861, and was expanded in use under Sultan Abdulaziz.

2 Unknown, 1850.
3 Sevket, 1907.

FRENCH ZOUAVE UNIFORM DEVELOPMENT AND ADOPTION

Development of the French Zouave uniform begins with France's 1er Regiment des Zouaves created in 1852 in the province of Algiers, and the distinctive Zouave uniform can be traced to the 1853 French Army regulations. The unit's origin dates back to 1830, with the French annexation of Algeria. The distinctive uniform's popularity was largely due to its novel attraction, and conduct of the Soldiers who wore it, were so admired that the Sardinian Bersaglieri adopted the Fez as a fatigue cap from the French Zouave they met during the Crimean War[4].

Adoption in the Turkish Army in 1861, were driven by a variety of influences. Key elements of the French Zouave uniform directly reflected garments commonly worn in the Ottoman Empire by its citizens, going back to the late-18th Century:

> "All the Turks wear turbans, loose jackets, short pantaloons, Morocco slippers, and a sash round the waist, in which they constantly carry a long dagger and a brace of pistols ... Their heads are close shaved, and covered by a small scull-cap, which is hidden under the turban."[5]

Adoption of the French Zouave uniform by the Turkish Army in 1861, was in large part an attempt to harken back to its traditional origins. It was observed by commentators in the 1860s, that:

> "the old Infantry dress, seen in the museum of ancient costumes at Constantinople, a man could march lightly, breathe freely, and sleep comfortably; the desiderata which ought to predominate in the mind of every designer of a military garb. The reigning ... [Sultan Abdulaziz] ... soon after his accession sagaciously flattered the national taste and increased with self-respect the efficiency of his troops, by the re-adoption of an oriental cut uniform."[6]

The clothing-uniforms of the Ottoman Spahis: Cavalry, and the Janissary common in the 1800s consisting of a collarless long-sleeved jersey and short waistcoat, combined with Russian pants, and waist wrap; likewise reflected essential elements of the later French Zouave uniform. Historical elements such as these, made the uniform appealing. Its use in the Turkish Army from 1861 onwards, also reflected French influence from the Crimean War (where they first encountered the Zouave). The Turkish Army adopted a uniform that was a near direct copy of the 1853 French Army regulations.

1853 FRENCH ARMY REGULATION ZOUAVE UNIFORM

The 1853 French Army regulations establishing the Zouave uniform proscribed a collarless Arabic-styled, or Bolero jacket, in dark blue cloth (sky-blue for the Algerian Riflemen), with a 12 millimetres wide madder (dark red) wool tape edging. The jacket's front panels were adorned with an Arabesque Daffodil made from the same 12 millimetres tape as the edging. The pattern finished with a three-leaf clover, which terminated around the wearer's collarbone area. More elaborate Arabesque, braid, applique and embroidery was sometimes added around the basic tape decorations. The lower end of the Daffodil pattern formed into a loop enclosing an area, called a pocket (there are versions where this is an actual small fob-pocket). The enclosed area was distinctively coloured. This was used to identify each of the Zouave Infantry Regiments. In the case of the Turkish Army the pockets were coloured red for the Chasseur A'Pied (their title in French): Nisanci (Marksmen) Battalions, and the 1st Imperial Guard Infantry Regiment, or light blue for the Artillery. For the rest of the Soldiers wearing the Zouave uniform, the pockets remained the base colour of the jacket. No attempt was made to use the pocket colour as a means to distinguish individual Regiments from each other.

Classically, the French Zouave Arabic-styled, or Bolero jacket typically ends well above, or at the waistline. The front is cut wide-open, and tends not to be joined or buttoned together at all. Some versions – as the front panels angle-up, join-up at the top and incorporate a top hook and eye used to close the jacket at the collar, leaving the rest flowing away to the sides, with the underlying shirt

---

4 Esposito, 2017.
5 Walsh, 1803.
6 Slade, 1867.

or vest showing. As the jacket ends well above, or at the waistline, a broad waist wrap is usually incorporated to cover the waist, as well as secure the broad bloomer pants.

The French Zouave Arabic-styled, or Bolero jacket was worn over a collarless and sleeveless vest made from blue cloth and edged with the same tape as the jacket. The tape border ran around the collar, down the front of the vest, and around the base, and arm holes. The vest opened under one of the arms, to allow the wearer to put it on, and was closed by a line of small bone buttons.

The pointed cuff on the French Zouave uniform, and a tunic version often used by Officers, was modified with a button edged back cuff-slit running up to the elbow. This appears as a band of wide tape edging the base of the cuff, and running along the back-seam edges, one side of which is edged with a line of buttons, that in some versions are left permanently open, and in other versions have a corresponding row of cord loops, to close the sleeve around the cuff.

▲ French Zouave, Sardinian Bersaglieri and British Soldiers during the Crimean War[7].

---

7 Garnier, 1856.

ZOUAOUA BERBER TRIBAL INFANTRY

The Zouaoua Berber Tribe originally inhabited the coastal mountain Djurdjura region of North Africa, and traditionally this Tribe provided warriors and mercenary troops in service to the Dey: the Ottoman ruler of Algeria. In the Ottoman Empire's military system prior to 1826, in North Africa, the Zouaoua Berber had a considerable military presence as their Soldiers were provided in substantial numbers to all of the Barbary States. The Dey of Algeria had several Battalions traditionally organized on the same basis as the rest of the Ottoman pre-1826 Orta: Musketeer Battalion, of approximately 1,000 soldiers each. The Tunisians, before and after their military reforms of 1831, incorporated several Regiments of Zouaoua, and these were organized into Tunisian Army Brigades of 1,000 to 2,000 Soldiers each[8]. In Ottoman Libya, likewise the Army there was dependent on Arab and Berber Auxiliaries. Even in Egypt, the Berber Infantry was a significant part of the Ottoman military structure there. A significant recognition of these troops' military effectiveness, the commander of the French Expeditionary Force which occupied Algeria recommended in August 1830, the continued employment of the Zouaoua, raising first a Battalion, then a second unit after this.

1830 FRENCH ZOUAVE UNIFORMS

In 1830, with French annexation of Algeria, its Government quickly collapsed, and the Zouaoua were persuaded to provide Soldiers for the French Army's interior campaign. By 1833, two battalions had been formed, now called Zouaves by the French, raised specifically as Colonial Troops. Later opened-up to French Soldiers who eventually became the 1st, and later Zouave Regiments in the French Army of North Africa. The early uniform is shown in a late-19th to early-20th Century illustration of a figure titled: Officier de Zouaves en Costume Orient (1830-1834): Zouaves Officer in Orient Costume[9]; and another set of figures from 1931 of the, "Chasseurs d'Afrique 1832: Officier et Soldat, C. des Indigenes"[10]; and, "7er Bon. de Zouaves 1834: Tambour and Lieutenant"[11.] This shows how the early uniforms appear to have been quite similar to the final pattern established in the 1853 French Army regulation Zouave uniform[12]. It also has a strong relationship to the earlier Napoleonic Period Mameluke Cavalry. The figure wears a large, patterned turban, a highly gold embroidered collarless blue Bolero jacket pattern with a much lower cut, reaching down to the waist, and front panels with broad square ends, which reveal a collarless vest covering the chest. Russian pants reaching down to the ground, and broad waist sash complete the dress. In the background, Soldiers wearing Zouave uniforms are depicted wearing versions similar to the final form adopted by 1853 in the French Army.

The relationship with the uniforms worn by the Algerian Zouaoua Berber Tribe Soldiers has some parallels, but also marked differences. For instance, one depiction of a Kabyle: Berber Infantryman of Algeria or Tunisia, from around the 1840s[13], depicts these Bedouin warriors wearing long white loose-fitting shirts, Fez-styled caps, and open-toed sandals with tied cords wrapped around their bare calves. Whereas, a number of Emir Abdelkader [Abdel-Kaders] Period Soldiers (who fought the French invasion in Algeria, up till 1847)[14][15], show several similar uniform characteristics to the French Zouave version as this was developing in its early years.

---

8 Mallett, 2013.
9 Breville, 1898.
10 Boisselier, 1931.
11 Boisselier, 1931.
12 Charles, 1860.
13 Rigo, 1840.
14 Unknown, 1843.
15 Unknown, 1847.

A short loose fitting jacket with hood that could be worn up over the head, or left loose hanging from the back collar seam. Made in blue, red, grey and black wool cloth, also appearing in dark grey-green cloth, and decorated in tape-trim, as well as traditional tribal designs. The jacket could be buttoned-up, using a row of small seam buttons, and loops (whereas the Zouave Bolero jacket pattern is open-to-the-front). Under the jacket a collarless sleeveless vest, typically seen in Algeria or Tunisia at the time, was often elaborately embroidered, and used wide tape and rows of small buttons and loops to close the front reaching the collar.

Knee length broad bloomer pants worn by the Zouaoua Infantry were extremely full-cut, to the point that large extra-folds of lose fabric collected between the leg holes. The leg holes were edged in tape, possibly to hold a draw string, to close the holes around the legs just below the knees. Other than that the Zouaoua wore no leggings as was common among Ottoman Empire citizens, and Turkish Soldiers throughout the 18th and 19th Centuries, and were bare-legged except for yellow leather slippers on their feet.

The Zouaoua typically wore a small rounded red wool felt cap with a small tuft at the top, commonly called the Greek cap in this period, and some accounts testify that Soldiers could wear up to three of these at a time, one over the other, with the brims folded up. This was also worn alongside early low unlined felt versions of the red Turkish Fez. In the case of the French Zouave uniform, from the early-1830s, an unlined red wool felt version of the Fez was used, with a long tassel hanging from a cord, and worn with a turban.

NAPOLEON'S MAMELUKE CAVALRY

A photograph taken in 1857, or 1858 of Corporal Ducel, who had served in the Mameluke de la Garde between 1813, and 1815 shows close parallels with many contemporary French uniforms in the Napoleonic Period made in the Turkish-style[16]. Key uniform elements typical to the early French uniform of the Orient, was a high collared sleeved jersey (that was closed to the collar with buttons). This was often worn in conjunction with an unbuttoned, except for a collar hook-and-eye, winged sleeveless waist coat, cut as a Bolero jacket. Incorporating Russian pants, commonly worn by Cossack and Ottomans alike, to complete the Mameluke-look. The end of the French Campaign in Egypt, saw the arrival of the original Mameluke in France to form their Cavalry Squadron for the French Army. They wore a tall red conical Ottoman hat, common in the Ottoman Cavalry at the time called a Cahouk, with a turban. Interestingly, we can see one of the first alterations to Turkish dress in France in this period, when Napoleon issued a decree dictating that the Mameluke hat should be green. The Ducel uniform shows that by the end of the Napoleonic Wars, the headdress had evolved into a green cloth covered peakless Shako with a turban wrapped around it.

LITHUANIAN TARTAR SQUADRON

The 1812 till 1814 Lithuanian Tartar Squadron was one squadron attached to Konopka's 3rd Lancer Regiment of the Imperial Guard. Created at Vilna on 8 October, 1812, and raised from largely Muslim descendants of Genghis Khan settled in Lithuania, during the Middle Ages. The Lithuanian Tartar uniform consisted of a high-collar buttoned sleeved jersey, which was worn under an unbuttoned (except for a collar hook-and-eye), winged-sleeve waist coat, cut as a Bolero jacket. This had a lower cut, reaching down to the waist, and had side panels with broad square ends, all edged with tape, and embroidered work. Like the uniform of the French Army Mameluke, the Lithuanian Tartar Squadron uniform made use of Russian pants. A Busby was worn to complete the dress.

---

16 Ducel, 1860.

THE FRENCH MAMELUKE CRAZE

Napoleon's invasion of Egypt set-off a Mameluke craze in Parisian fashion, reflecting well known oriental or Turkish-styles; notwithstanding the clothing was more fantasy than reality. Interestingly, when a Mameluke noble – Captain Ibrahim was lost on his first visit to Paris, during Napoleon's First Consulate Period, he was confronted by a jeering aggressive crowd ridiculing his strange clothing, shouting: 'it was not carnival time, so why was he wearing Turkish costume?'. Fearing for his life, Captain Ibrahim shot two of the men in the crowd dead[17]. In France during the First Consulate, the Mameluke who had joined the French Army, wore mostly their Egyptian clothing, which differed greatly from the later dress developed under Napoleon, which Ducel's Mameluke de la Garde uniform is illustrative. During the First Consulate, the Mameluke started to received uniforms issues that ultimately developed into the French Army's Mameluke (and later Uniform of the Orient). Initially, they wore a Yelek: a short Turkish waist-length coat, which was worn open over the waist sash. This had wide sleeves, and was fur trimmed. They still wore a wrap-around Turkish shirt, which left the upper chest and neck exposed. This was also worn along-side a shirt which was cut round at the neck, and collarless.

Later, French Army Musicians could be seen wearing a Mameluke-style of uniform[18]. Even Napoleon's personal attendant - Saint-Denis; Napoleon insisted that he be dress as a Mameluke, and gave him the name of Ali (Mameluke Ali), and he wore exactly the same clothing as the rest of the Mameluke in the French Army. During the Greek Revolution, the 1828 French Expedition de Moree, in Greek Service, its French Officers leading the troops soon adopted for themselves, much of the common dress of Greek Soldiers they encountered, including short jackets near identical to the Bolero.

The basic transition that occurred between the Napoleonic Period and the later French Zouave uniform, was a reversal of the pattern, moving the sleeves from the underlying collared jersey (which had been adopted for the Napoleonic Mameluke uniform), and fitting these onto the short jacket (previously the over vest). In the case of the later Zouave uniform the underlying jersey was retained, and turned more into a true vest. The vest's closure/buttoning arrangement was located under one of the arms, even though most versions of the French Zouave vest have tape decoration running down the chest giving the appearance of a closure seam.

European Orientalists, ethnographic and military artists exhibiting in the Salons from the early-1830s, popularised Turkish Irregular Soldiers, in the familiar Bolero–styled jackets, Russian pants, waist sashes, Fez and turban - all of which were the key elements shared with the later French Zouave uniform. In closing, the real origin of the Zouave uniform was French imagining of the appearance of the Soldier of the Orient created in the early years of the Napoleonic Wars and revitalised in the early-1830s during the Campaign in North Africa. Its arrival in the Ottoman Empire – during a time otherwise known as the Zouave-craze of the 1860s, saw many countries including the North, and Confederacy, during the Civil War Period adopt this pattern of uniform.

TURKISH USE AND MANUFACTURE

The 1861 Era Turkish Army Zouave uniform was nearly identical to the 1853 French Army regulation version. A surviving example of the 1861 Era Turkish Army Zouave jacket is known in a museum collection, and it is dark blue, with red tape decorations, and cuffs[19]. The pointed cuffs appear wider than seen on the French version of the Zouave jacket. Above each cuff an additional red tape cuff chevron has been added. The Bolero jacket has a high-cut waist line, stopping around the wearer's elbows. The bottom front corners are rounded, and top (collar corners) are more square-ended. The edge has red piping all around.

---

17 Pawly, 2012.

18 Boisselier, 1959.

19 Askeri Muze, 2017.

▲ Early-1861 Turkish Zouave jacket with a high-cut waist line. An alternative back version is shown. Later versions had lower-cut waist-lines.

The museum collection version has a narrow blue gap (the underlying jacket cloth), and then there is a wider red tape running all-around the jacket edge. A red piping sleeve seam can be seen on each shoulder. The front panels do not close, and are cut far-apart. The Arabesque Daffodil design was identical to the French version. The trefoil knot is upwards facing, and is positioned on the wearer's shoulder area. The pockets are left unfilled. Line Infantry used this jacket type. The back of the jacket was either plain, or two vents were cut, that were also fully edged in tape, these helped open the jacket getting it on, or off. A 1907 illustration[20], and 19th Century colourized lithograph[21], show that the bottom edge of the jacket could be cut lower than the museum version. The version shown in the 19th Century colourized lithograph, is for a Horse Artillery Bascavus: Sergeant-Major and had much more elaborate Arabesque braid, applique, embroidery and tape decoration.

The 1861 Era Turkish Army Zouave jacket was a copy of the French Army version, but was not imported from France in any large numbers. The surviving museum collection example, when compared to French versions shows different overall construction. The 1861 Turkish version of the Zouave uniform was made in red, as well as dark blue cloth, and there were yellow and green tape variations. It was adopted for use by the: 1st and 2nd Imperial Guard Infantry Regiments; 1st Ordu: Army Line Infantry Regiments; all the Chasseur A'Pied (their title in French): Nisanci (Marksmen) Battalions; Imperial Guard Cavalry Regiments, all the Artillery, and Navy Infantry.

---

20 Sevket, 1907.
21 Roubicek, 1978.

THE 1861 ERA TURKISH ZOUAVE UNIFORMS DETAILS ARE SET OUT IN THE FOLLOWING TABLE:

UNIT	Jacket	Cuff	Tape	Pocket	Pants	Special Distinctions
1st Imperial Guard Infantry	Dark Blue	Dark Blue	Yellow	Red	Red	Yellow Fez Tassel White Turban Blue Waist Band Yellow Pants Piping
2nd Imperial Guard Infantry	Dark Blue	Red	Red	Dark Blue	Red	Green Turban Blue Waist Band
1st Ordu: Army Line Infantry	Dark Blue	Red	Red	Dark Blue	Dark Blue	Red Shoulder Piping Red Waist Band Red Pants Piping
Chasseur A'Pied Battalions	Dark Blue	Dark Blue	Green	Red	Dark Blue	Green Pants Piping Red Waist Band
Gendarmery Regiments	Light Blue	Light Blue	Yellow	Red	Light Blue	Red Waist Band
1st Imperial Guard Cavalry	Red	Dark Blue	Yellow	Red	Dark Blue	Red Waist Band Yellow Cuff Tape Red Cuff Base
2nd Imperial Guard Cavalry	Red	Dark Blue	Yellow	Red	Dark Blue	Red Waist Band Yellow Cuff Tape Red Cuff Base
3rd Cavalry	Dark Blue	Dark Blue	Red	Dark Blue	Dark Blue	Red Waist Band
4th Cavalry	Dark Blue	Dark Blue	Red	Dark Blue	Dark Blue	Red Waist Band
Field Artillery Horse Artillery	Dark Blue	Dark Blue	Red	Light Blue	Dark Blue	Red Shoulder Piping Red Waist Band Red
Navy Infantry	Dark Blue	Red	Red	Dark Blue	Dark Blue	Red Waist Band Red Pants Piping

After 1876, the French Zouave Infantry uniform was retained by one regiment of Imperial Guard Infantry, as well as by the Redif: Reserve Infantry, which received the uniforms as surplus from the Nizam: Regular Line Infantry, and Artillery. In 1914, old surplus 1861 Zouave uniforms were still being worn by the Ottoman Gendarmery in Lebanon. During WW1, the last Soldiers to wear the Zouave uniform was the Camel Raiders who adopted a distinctive field brown Zouave-styled uniform, and commonly wore this over a wool or cotton cloth pull-over jersey, this was even completed with a grey cloth waist wrap. Other Camel Riders, are known to have worn a version of the collarless Zouave–styled vest, which buttoned-up at the shoulder seam on one side. It was manufactured in green and/or brown cloth. This was commonly worn with a scarf, or neck-wrap.

NATIONAL FEZ

The 1832 decree of Sultan Mahmud II, declared the Fez to be the national headdress, to be worn by civilians and military alike. The new bonnet worn by Mahmud II and his troops was the crimson wool Fez; traditionally made in places such as the south of France, Tunis, or by Tunisians living in Constantinople, and had long been worn in the Mediterranean, and North Africa. It was seen as early, as 1669 worn by Ottoman troops at the siege of Candia. The pre-1807, Nizam-i-Cedid: New Order Army Soldiers of Sultan Selim III commonly wore the Janissary red skull cap, as well as the traditional tall red caps of the Boustangees, both of which are regarded as forerunners to the adoption of the Fez. In 1827, an order was made for 50,000 tall cylindrical red hats from Tunis, by the Sultan for the newly established Army, and these were modified with the addition of yellow tape stripes. On 3 March 1829, new laws were passed regulating the dress of several ranks of Imperial Officials, and this included the use of these tall red hats. In 1832, the Imperial Fez Factory was established at Eyup, employing Tunisian, Turkish and Armenians to make the new Fez which by this stage had added an enormous tassel, which was not reduced in bulk till 1845[22]. Crimean War commentators describe the standard Army Fez as red, with a dark blue tassel[23]. Early Fez tassels were much larger, and more voluminous than later versions, and required regular hair dressing in Constantinople barber's shops. In the Crimean War Period, commonly the Military Fez had the addition of a brass button, plate or rosette securing the tassels:

> "The Soldiers of the Turkish Army, and … Navy, have a small circular plate of polished brass fixed upon the summit of the Fez. This plate is a distinctive mark of the Imperial Military and Naval Service."[24]

Special orders, given to the 4th Ordu: Army of Anatolia, in 1854, that the tassel of the Fez was in future to be worn on the left side over the ear. It was also known that the Cavalry version of the Military Fez had a chin strap fitted[25].

The 1861 Era Turkish Army and Navy continued with the tradition of wearing the Fez, as the national headdress. An actual military version had disappeared, and the Army and Navy took to wearing the civil version. However, the 1st Imperial Guard Regiment as a special distinction were given yellow tassels, and the 2nd Imperial Guard Regiment wrapped a green turban around their Fez. The Fez took-on a much lower conical shape, and commonly the tassel was secure to the top, by a long length of cord, which allowed it to hang much further down the back of the head. The red wool felt fabric covered Fez was lined, and stiffened inside with cardboard or woven cane base, with a leather sweat band sewn in place. This was also worn alongside early low unlined felt versions of the Turkish Fez. Not all were impressed by the Fez, as one 1858 British Government report commented, like the rest of the Soldier's uniform, it became soiled, and was typically not cleaned:

> "when the Fez has become pale or clouded, and the tassel, almost devoid of colour, hangs dishevelled beneath the dimmed brass".[26]

The 1861 Era Fez was plain, and only the Gardes du Palais wore a star and crescent badge on it with a plume. Not all 1861 Era Soldiers wore the Fez, as the Busby was worn by the Gardes du Palais, the Cossacks, Circassien Volunteer Cavalry Squadron, and the Kazakhstan Cavalry, who wore a low lambswool cap. The only other variation was some Navy Soldiers wore the Greek hat.

---

22 Mansel, 2005.
23 Norman, 1985.
24 Radcliffe, 1858.
25 Norman. 1985.
26 Radcliffe, 1858.

C.Flaherty

FIGURE 1: Napoleonic Period French Army Mameluke de la Garde.
FIGURE 1a: French Army Musician in a Turkish uniform (1811).
FIGURE 1b: Abdel-Kaders Infantry Soldier in Algiers (1847).
FIGURE 2a: A French Zouave Infantry Soldier (1860).

CHAPTER 1: ARMY ORGANIZATION AND INFANTRY

INTRODUCTION

The 1861 Era, saw several changes in the Army. The general structure of the Army was preserved as it had been in the Crimean War Period, however, the Hassa lost much of its independent status around 1861. The Hassa origin began as the Sultan's Household Infantry, it was only formalised into an Imperial Guard along western lines after 1826, when Sultan Mahmud II reformed the Boustangees [Bostangis; Bostandji] into the Muallem Bostansyan-i-Hassa: Trained Imperial Gardeners[27]. From 1826 till 1841, the Hassa incorporated two Foot Regiments, of three Battalions of 900 Soldiers each, composed of the Boustangees[28]. After 1841, the Hassa Imperial Guard Corps was transferred into the newly formed 1st Ordu, Khass-Ssa [Hassa Ordusu]: Imperial Guard Army, headquartered in Constantinople[29][30].

The 1861 changes treated the Hassa as like the other Ordu: Armies, being renamed the 1st Dersaadet Ordu: Army[31]. This had been the title of a second Ordu: Army: 2nd Ordu Army Deri-Seadat: Constantinople and Adjoining Districts of Europe and Asia, which is known from an 1852 organization chart, based on the 1843, and 1848 Turkish Army Organization Laws, that had established the Ordu: Armies[32][33]. The Hassa still retained its former prestige, as the seven Infantry Regiments continued to serve as the Imperial Guards. The second major change was raising of the 7th Yemen Ordu: Army, sometime between 1861 and 1876, that had its Headquarters in Sana'a (the largest city in Yemen)[34]. The new Ordu: Army, "was needed to deal with both continuous rebellions and with the increasingly important Red Sea Straits (in order to control navigation by the British and French into the region)."[35]

THE 1846, AND 1861 TRANSITION TO THE FIELD ORDU: ARMIES[36]:

1846 – CRIMEAN WAR ORDU: ARMIES	1861 ORDU: ARMIES
1st Ordu Khass-Ssa [Hassa Ordusu]: Imperial Guard Army Western Border of Asia Minor	1st Dersaadet Ordu: Army in Constantinople
2nd Ordu: Army Deri-Seadat: Constantinople and Adjoining Districts of Europe and Asia	2nd Tuna Ordu: Army in Sumnu
3rd Ordu: Army Rumeli	3rd Rumeli Ordu: Army in Manastir
4th Ordu: Army Anadolis [Anatolian], Turkey	4th Anadolu Ordu: Army in Erzurum
5th Ordu: Army Ababistan, Syria	5th Suriye Ordu: Army in Damascus
6th Ordu: Army Irak, Mesopotamia and Cerobia	6th Arabistan Ordu: Army in Baghdad
	7th Yemen Ordu: Army in Sana'a

---

27 Shaw, 1977.
28 Roubicek, 1978.
29 Shaw, 1977.
30 Roubicek, 1978.
31 Uyar, 2009.
32 Urquhart, 1852.
33 Roubicek, 1978.
34 Roubicek, 1978.
35 Uyar, 2009.
36 Uyar, 2009.

INFANTRY REGIMENT NUMBERS AND TERRITORIAL NAMES

Infantry Regiments, following the 1843, and 1848 Turkish Army Organization Laws were numbered from one to six within each Ordu: Army, along with names of places where they were stationed[37][38]. The system continued during the 1861 Era.

1861 TILL 1876 ORDU: ARMIES 1-7 COMPOSITION (AND ALTERNATIVE TERRITORIAL DESIGNATIONS)

1ST DERSAADET ORDU: ARMY; 1ST CONSTANTINOPLE ORDU: ARMY HASSA			
INFANTRY	6 Regiments	3 Battalions Each	
CHASSEUR A'PIED		7 Battalions	
CAVALRY	5 Regiments	6 Squadrons Each	
COSSACK BRIGADE		8 Squadrons	
ARTILLERY	Line Regiment	9 Field Batteries	
		3 Horse Batteries	
IHTIYAT (1ST RESERVE)		12 Field Batteries	
	1 Mountain Battery		
ENGINEERS BRIGADE	4 Battalions	2 Companies Each:	Sappers Company
			Artificers Company

2ND TUNA ORDU: ARMY IN SUMNU; 2ND DANUBE ORDU: ARMY		
INFANTRY	6 Regiments	3 Battalions Each
FRONTIER REGIMENT		3 Battalions
CHASSEUR A'PIED		6 Battalions
CAVALRY	4 Regiments	6 Squadrons Each
ARTILLERY REGIMENT		12 Batteries
SAPPERS COMPANY		

3RD RUMELI ORDU: ARMY IN MANASTIR; 3RD ROUMELIA ORDU: ARMY		
INFANTRY	6 Regiments	3 Battalions Each
CHASSEUR A'PIED		7 Battalions
BOSNIAN BRIGADE	2 Regiments	3 Battalions Each
FRONTIER REGIMENT	Greek Border	3 Battalions
	Bosnian Border	4 Battalions
	Austro-Herzegovinian Battalion	
CAVALRY	4 Regiments	6 Squadrons Each
ARTILLERY REGIMENT		12 Batteries
	8 Mountain Batteries	
SAPPERS COMPANY		

4TH ANADOLU ORDU: ARMY IN ERZURUM; 4TH ANATOLIA ORDU: ARMY		
INFANTRY	4 Regiments	3 Battalions Each
	1 Regiment	1 Battalion
CHASSEUR A'PIED		6 Battalions
CAVALRY	3 Regiments	6 Squadrons Each
ARTILLERY REGIMENT		14 Batteries
SAPPERS COMPANY		

---

37 Urquhart, 1852.
38 Roubicek, 1978.

5TH SURIYE ORDU: ARMY IN DAMASCUS; 5TH SYRIA ORDU: ARMY		
INFANTRY	6 Regiments	3 Battalions Each
CHASSEUR A'PIED		7 Battalions
CAVALRY	4 Regiments	6 Squadrons Each
CAMEL CORPS		6 Squadrons
ARTILLERY REGIMENT		12 Batteries
SAPPERS COMPANY		
6TH ARABISTAN ORDU: ARMY IN BAGHDAD; 6TH BAGHDAD ORDU: ARMY		
INFANTRY	6 Regiments	3 Battalions Each
CHASSEUR A'PIED		6 Battalions
CAVALRY	2 Regiments	6 Squadrons Each
ARTILLERY REGIMENT		9 Batteries
7TH YEMEN ORDU: ARMY IN SANA'A; 7TH YEMEN ORDU: ARMY		
INFANTRY	5 Regiments	3 Battalions Each
CHASSEUR A'PIED		5 Battalions
CIRCASSIAN SQUADRON		
ARTILLERY REGIMENT		6 Batteries

INFANTRY TERRITORIAL TITLES (1846 TILL 1876)

1ST ORDU KHASS-SSA [HASSA ORDUSU]: IMPERIAL GUARD ARMY WESTERN BORDER OF ASIA MINOR ---------------------- 1ST DERSAADET ORDU: ARMY (1861-1876)	1st Imperial Guard Infantry Regiment Ismid
	2nd Imperial Guard Infantry Regiment Broussa
	3rd Infantry Regiment Smyrna
	4th Infantry Regiment Aidyn
	5th Infantry Regiment Kutayieh
	6th Infantry Regiment Sparta
2ND ORDU: ARMY DERI-SEADAT: CONSTANTINOPLE AND ADJOINING DISTRICTS OF EUROPE AND ASIA ---------------------- 2ND TUNA ORDU: ARMY IN SUMNU (1861-1876)	1st Infantry Regiment Adrianople
	2nd Infantry Regiment Shumla
	3rd Infantry Regiment Boli
	4th Infantry Regiment Angora
	5th Infantry Regiment Konia
	6th Infantry Regiment Kaisarieh
3RD ORDU: ARMY RUMELI ---------------------- 3RD RUMELI ORDU: ARMY IN MANASTIR (1861-1876)	1st Infantry Regiment Monastir
	2nd Infantry Regiment Tirhala
	3rd Infantry Regiment Selanik
	4th Infantry Regiment Uskup
	5th Infantry Regiment Sophia
	6th Infantry Regiment Wydin
4TH ORDU: ARMY ANADOLIS [ANATOLIAN], TURKEY ---------------------- 4TH ANADOLU ORDU: ARMY IN ERZURUM (1861-1876) (Lost one Infantry Regiment from 1861)	1st Infantry Regiment Sivas
	2nd Infantry Regiment Tocat
	3rd Infantry Regiment Kharput
	4th Infantry Regiment Erzerum
	5th Infantry Regiment Kars
	6th Infantry Regiment Diarbekir

5TH ORDU: ARMY ABABISTAN, SYRIA	1st Infantry Regiment Sham, Damascus
--------------------	2nd Infantry Regiment Balbek
	3rd Infantry Regiment Acre
5TH SURIYE ORDU: ARMY IN DAMASCUS (1861-1876)	4th Infantry Regiment Sidon
	5th Infantry Regiment Beyrut
	6th Infantry Regiment Haleb
6TH ORDU: ARMY IRAK, MESOPOTAMIA AND CEROBIA	1st Infantry Regiment Baghdad
	2nd Infantry Regiment Sulymanieh
--------------------	3rd Infantry Regiment Kerkuk
	4th Infantry Regiment Mossul
6TH ARABISTAN ORDU: ARMY IN BAGHDAD (1861-1876)	5th Infantry Regiment Jidda and Mecca
	6th Infantry Regiment Mokha and Massu [Masowah]

▲ The 1843, and 1848 Turkish Army Organization Laws established the following Infantry Regiments in each of the six Ordu: Armies[39][40]. Infantry retained these titles (these are in old spellings), throughout the era till 1878, when a new system of consecutive numbers was introduced. Territorial titles for the Yemen Infantry are not known.

INFANTRY REGIMENT ORGANIZATION AND UNIT STRENGTHS

The 1861 Era Infantry Regiment comprised two Battalions of eight Companies each[41]. The Battalion had 450 Officers and Soldiers in peacetime, and 800 in wartime, when it doubled its effective number by amalgamating with the local Redif: Reserve Infantry Soldiers that each Ordu: Army maintained. This practice was seen during the Crimean War Period. The 1869 Military Service Law doubled the number of Regiments each region had to provide[42]. Each recruitment region provided Soldiers for the Nizam: Regular Regiment, and two Redif Mouqaddam [Mukaddem] Battalions (effectively a second Regiment), two Redif Thaalee [Sani] Battalions (effectively a third Regiment), and a further two Saliss [Mustahfız; Moustahfeez]: Territorial Army Battalions (effectively a fourth Regiment).

The 1869 Military Service Law controlled a Soldier's life[43][44]. Recruited at the age of 20 years, an Infantry Soldier's Service Life with the Colours was four years in the Nizam: Regulars. The Soldier then spent another six years in the Redif: Reserve. Redif Service was divided into two parts: (1) Three years in the Mouqaddam [Mukaddem], this appears to have been an active service period; and, (2) Three years in the Thaalee [Sani], which was largely inactive service. The Soldier was then given eight years in the Saliss [Mustahfız; Moustahfeez]: Territorial Army. Discharged Regular Soldiers were usually assigned by the Military Administration to entirely separate Kism-i-Evvel: Redif Battalions, instead of mixing them together with raw Redif Soldiers[45]. Some young men aged 19 till 24 years, who were never chosen by the lottery to join the Nizam: Regular Army were instead enrolled directly into a war-service draft, for which they were liable to be called-up to, for the next 13 years[46].

---

39 Urquhart, 1852.
40 Roubicek, 1978.
41 Roubicek, 1978.
42 Uyar, 2009.
43 Roubicek, 1978.
44 Uyar, 2009.
45 Uyar, 2009.
46 Slade, 1867.

1861 TURKISH ARMY DETACHED TROOPS

The 1861 structure for the Fortress Commands, composed two Fortress Regions and 42 Fortresses, which had preserved their independent status with their own local troops. Independent Border Guard Battalions in the Bosnian, Greek, and Montenegrin regions were organized into three Independent Regiments[47].

DETACHED TROOPS	NUMBER OF REGIMENTS:	BATTALIONS-COMPANIES EACH:	
RESERVE ARTILLERY	1 Regiment	4 Battalions	3 Companies
GARRISON ARTILLERY	7 Regiments	4 Battalions	3 Companies
GARRISON ARTILLERY BATTALIONS		2 Battalions	4 Companies
MILITARY WORKMEN CORPS		42 Divisions	2 Battalions Each

The 1843 Turkish Army Organization Laws established two Regiments of Engineers under the Grand Master of Artillery[48]. It is known, they formed a, "Brigade of Engineers, about 1600 … [men]"[49]. The 1861 Era retained the Engineers Brigade as part of the 1st Ordu: Army in four Company Sappers, and Artificers Battalions. Along with these Soldiers, the 2nd, 3rd, 4th and 5th Ordu: Armies all had their own Sappers Companies.

The 1861 Era uniform worn by the Engineers Brigade, and the independent Sapper Companies was possibly the Infantry version of the Zouave uniform as this was newly expanded from its Crimean War Period organization.

CHASSEUR A'PIED: NISANCI (MARKSMEN) BATTALIONS

The original four to six Seshaneci: Foot Chasseur Battalions were formed under the 1843, and 1848 Turkish Army Organization Laws for each Ordu: Army[50][51]. From 1861, some 44 Chasseur A'Pied Battalions had been created and were distributed across the seven Ordu: Armies. The uniforms worn by the original Seshaneci: Foot Chasseur Battalions is still open to question. The most significant identifying feature was the troops' weapons and equipment. From 1852, Seshaneci: Foot Chasseur Battalions were armed with muzzle-loading rifles called: Seshane Tufegi[52]. Bought from France, these were the Minie 1851 rifled muskets, with sword-sabre bayonets. It is also known, that from August 1853, certain elite units were equipped with French and Belgian supplied Model 1849 Rifles, which had greater accuracy firing the Minie Ball[53]. Seshaneci: Foot Chasseur Battalions were also given the latest-version French Army waist belt equipment[54]. The 1861 Era Chasseur A'Pied Battalions Officer's uniform is known from a 1907 dated illustration: identified as an 'Officer in the Nisanci: Marksmen Battalions'. Depicted wearing a long skirted tunic with green collar and pointed cuffs[55]; the special distinction was retained after 1876[56]. The Chasseur A'Pied Soldiers uniform is also known from a 1907 dated illustration[57]. It shows a Zouave uniform, with the following distinctions:

---

47 Uyar, 2009.
48 Roubicek, 1978.
49 Dodd, 1856.
50 Roubicek, 1978.
51 Badem, 2010.
52 Zengin, 2015.
53 Bennett, 2018.
54 Norman, 1985.
55 Sevket, 1907.
56 Sevket, 1907.
57 Sevket, 1907.

BATTALIONS	Jacket	Cuffs	Tape	Pocket	Pants	Special Distinctions
Chasseur A'Pied	Dark Blue	Dark Blue	Green	Red	Dark Blue	Green Pants Piping Red Waist Band

The pants piping seen on the Chasseur A'Pied uniform, was based on the French Zouave version. An 1854 titled painting called: Zouaves[58], shows the pants were provided with large-sized side seam pockets edged in piping forming rings, which continued down the leg. Additional piping lines ran down on either side.

IMPERIAL GUARD INFANTRY REGIMENTS

The 1861 French Zouaves uniform for the 1st Imperial Guard is known from a 1907 illustration, showing they wore yellow distinctions[59]. This was a continuation of a Soldier, in a completely yellow uniform, argued to have been from the Solak Imperial Guard Orta, trained as a new battalion in the pre-1807 Nizam-i-Cedid: New Order Army Soldiers of Sultan Selim III (1789-1807); these Guardsmen then became the Yellow Regiment in the 1826 New Mansure Army, formed under Abdul Mahmud II, which continued till 1832-39, with the Regiment's distinction of yellow jackets and Fez tassels.

The 2nd Imperial Guard uniform is also known from a 1907 illustration, showing red distinctions[60]. Distinctively the Fez was wrapped in a green turban. The significance of the green keffiyeh at the time, '[denoted] … a man who has religious privileges"[61]. It is open to question as to what religious privileges reserved specifically to the 2nd Imperial Guard; however, it may have been associated with the Selamlik: the Topkapi Palace public reception area where the Sultan received his guests. One of the functions, performed there by Soldiers taken from various elite units in Constantinople, was water-carrying and distribution for a Selamlik purification ceremony performed by the guests.

INFANTRY REGIMENTS	Jacket	Cuffs	Tape	Pocket	Pants	Special Distinctions
1st Imperial Guard	Dark Blue	Dark Blue	Yellow	Red	Red	Yellow Fez Tassel, White Turban Blue Waist Band, Yellow Pants Piping
2nd Imperial Guard	Dark Blue	Red	Red	Dark Blue	Red	Green Turban Blue Waist Band

INFANTRY ZOUAVE UNIFORM

Possibly from early in 1861, and relating to the final year of Sultan Abdulmecid, an illustration titled: Turkey Infanterie [Infantry][62], shows a possible early version of a Zouave uniform, as it is related to another illustration, which shows the same Soldiers wearing Crimean War Period equipment cross-belts[63]. This version – possibly only in use for a short time, before the later 1861 versions was adopted. The figure wears a plain dark blue Bolero jacket edged in yellow tape, with red pointed cuffs, with a yellow tape top edge. The vest has a red tape centre-line, and the open collar is edged with red tape. The wide waist sash is red. Wide light blue bloomer pants, and black high calf boots complete the dress. The 1861 Zouave uniform adopted for the four Infantry Regiments numbered 3rd to 6th, in the 1st Ordu: Army, appears to have been exactly the same for all according to a 1907 illustration[64], and surviving one in a museum collection for a Line Infantry Soldier[65]. The Line Infantry wore red cuff distinctions:

---

58 Unknown, 1854.
59 Sevket, 1907.
60 Sevket, 1907.
61 War Office, 2008.
62 Unknown, 1850.
63 Unknown, 1850.
64 Sevket, 1907.
65 Askeri Muze, 2017.

REGIMENT(S)	Jacket	Cuffs	Tape	Pocket	Pants	Special Distinctions
3rd Infantry	Dark Blue	Red	Red	Dark Blue	Dark Blue	Red Shoulder Piping
4th Infantry						Red Waist Band
5th Infantry						Red Pants Piping
6th Infantry						

INFANTRY TUNIC

The Zouave uniform was issued to recently raised, or reorganized specific units in the Turkish Army. It is largely inferred that the remaining Line Infantry continued to make do with the tunic. Actual evidence for the 1853 Infantry Soldier's tunic continued use after 1861 is virtually non-existent except for the example worn by the Garde du Palais: Imperial Palace Guard Company. The standard Army tunic was called the 'New Uniform' by Crimean War commentators. Dating to around 1853, it was a universal pattern dark blue tunic with seven to eight (depending on the wearer's height) brass crescent buttons down the front, with a short skirt. The standard 1853 Turkish Army tunic was straight cut, and resembled the later British pattern tunic introduced at the end of the Crimean War, around 1856. The skirt length typically was cut short below the cuff, with flapped round cuffs, and no rear pocket flaps, except for a rear vent ending in two rear-waist buttons. The Crimean War tunic was trimmed with red tape down the tunic front, along the collar edge, edging the cuffs, and its square-ended shoulder boards.

The Egyptian Army, in the 1877 Russo-Turkish War, appeared in a low rounded collared, loose-cut version of the Crimean War tunic, with a lower collar, and pointed cuffs. The Egyptian Army tunic was dark blue with white piping, and closed by six buttons. Loose dark blue pants, with white piped seams, were tucked into white caff leggings, with black shoes[66]. The 1877 Egyptian Soldier is depicted wearing a red cuff chevron to show their rank, that of an Onbasi: Corporal. As the Egyptian Army tended to follow Turkish Army uniform changes its tunic design was similar.

The 1861 Era Turkish Army tunic's main change was to adopt pointed cuffs. This was required by the new rank system that used cuff chevrons by both Officers, and Junior Officers to identify individual ranks.

The Crimean War Period Soldier's tunic was fitted with shoulder boards with red Ottoman numerals for Infantry Regiments one to six, in each Ordu: Army. The practice likely continued throughout the 1861 Era, for Infantry who still wore a tunic. Consecutive numbering of Turkish Army Infantry Regiments was not introduced until 1878[67].

INFANTRY WHITE SMOCK

Extracted from a larger illustration, titled: Ottoman Army Soldiers during the 1877 Russo-Turkish War[68], two figures of Turkish Soldiers are depicted wearing a white smock, not unlike the French colonial service white fatigue uniform of the time. The Infantry Soldier's white fatigue uniform consisted of a low open collared garment that was closed by a short vent with two large buttons. The shirt cuffs were also closed

▲ This later 1878 gilt metal Army tunic button shows the 1861 type used on tunics. A lesser-known variation of the more common star and crescent type.

66 Drury, 2012.
67 Cox, 1997.
68 Ollier, 1890.

around the wrist with a button. The front of the smock was heavily pleated. The smock hem came down to the wearer's calves. Loose white pants, and waist band completed the dress.

GREATCOATS

Possibly, from early-1861, and relating to the final year of Sultan Abdulmecid, illustrations of Turkish Infantry show Zouave uniform and a greatcoat, along with Crimean War Period equipment cross-belts. The illustration depicts the greatcoat as a French-styled version in medium blue, with a red high collar, and straight cuffs. Single breasted with seven, to eight buttons, the skirt is shown buttoned back. A type of mantle-cloak is also depicted in a 1907 illustration, with a hood, and based on French Zouave uniform types[69]. This was in blue cloth, with red trim, and closed over the chest with a cord toggle. Another 1870s Turkish Army Zouave-style hooded mantle is known in a museum collection, it is dark blue cloth, trimmed in red tape, and was closed with three toggle cords across the chest[70]. Each toggle had a large cloth multi-pointed star backing.

STOCKINGS, BOOTS AND SPATS

In the Crimean War Period a wide variety of footwear was used. The 1861 Era sees introduction for the Army as a whole, the French-styled Zouave uniform combination of yellow wool stockings, and black shoes covered by a white calf spat. The Turkish version of the spat used a white top securing strap[71], the French version was commonly black.

FIGURE 3: Crimean War Period set of Soldier's tunic shoulder boards with Ottoman numerals for Infantry Regiments one to six in each Ordu: Army.
FIGURE 4: Star and crescent tunic button.
FIGURE 5: Crescent tunic button.
FIGURE 6: Line Infantry wearing a post-1861 version of the tunic.
FIGURE 7: French Zouave Infantry uniform.
FIGURE 8: Infantry tunic and Zouave jacket cuff details and back view.
FIGURE 9: Soldier's Zouave-styled overcoat.
FIGURE 9a: Overcoat breast stars and toggle-loops.
FIGURE 10: Chasseur A'Pied Soldier.
FIGURE 10a: Pants pocket details.
FIGURE 11: 1st Imperial Guard Infantry Regiment.
FIGURE 12: 2nd Imperial Guard Infantry Regiment.
FIGURE 13: Turkish Infantry early version of the Zouave uniform.
FIGURE 13a: Zouave vest.
FIGURE 13b: Infantry Summer Dress.

69 Sevket, 1907.
70 Askeri Muze, 2017.
71 Sevket, 1907.

▼ An 1877 Egyptian Infantry Soldier wearing the tunic.

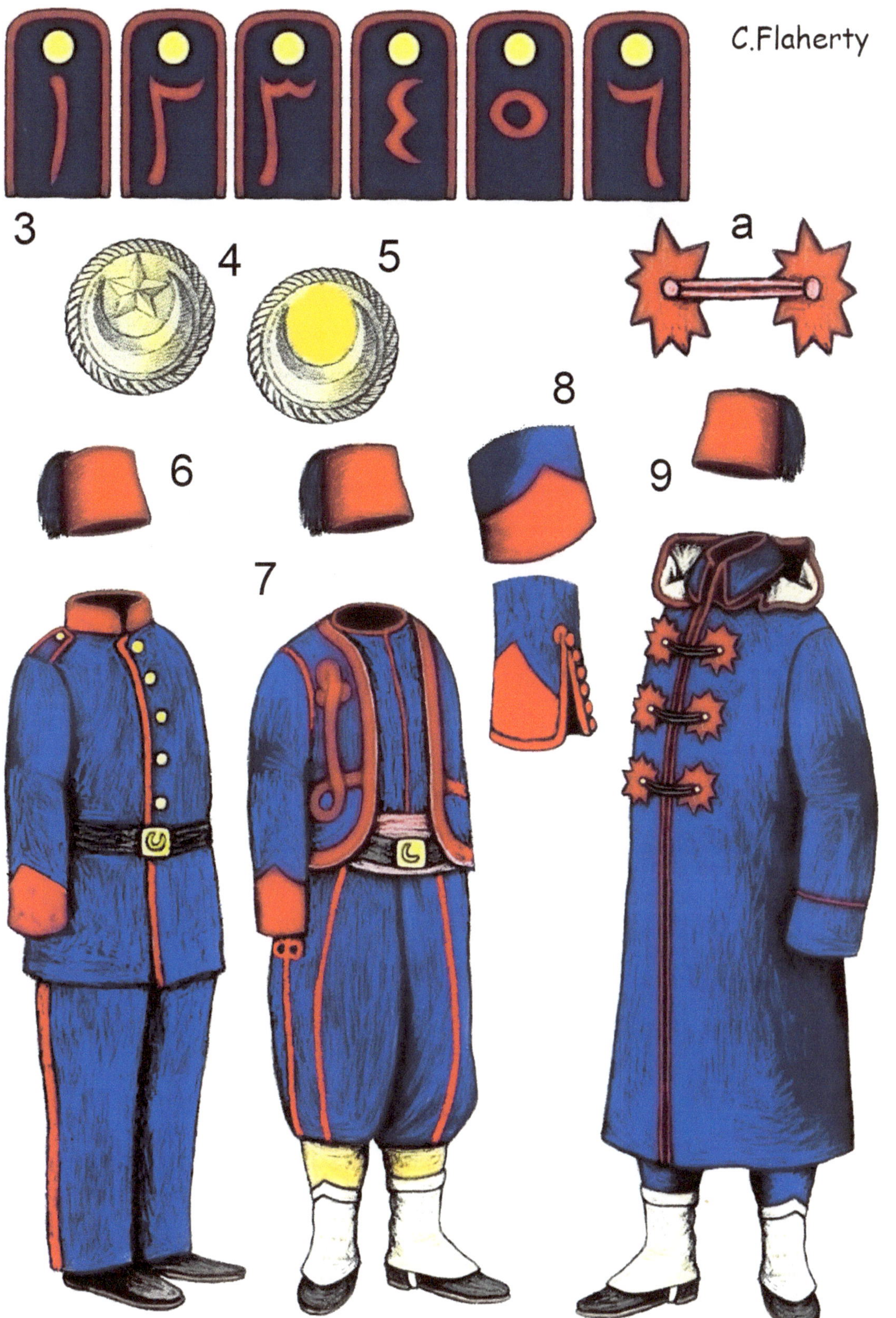

C.Flaherty
3
4
5
a
6
7
8
9

C.Flaherty

CHAPTER 2: RANK INSIGNIA AND OFFICER'S UNIFORMS

INTRODUCTION

The notable change for the Army from 1861 onwards, was adoption of a consistent system of rank identification based on gold or silver cuff chevrons. By the end of the Era, the insignia had become French-styled trefoil sleeve knots. Prior to that, Officers' ranks bands were distinguished by three grades of gold epaulettes, and by the fringe type used:

Senior Officer (Generals)	Rigid fringed
Mid-Level Officers (Colonel, Lieutenant-Colonel, Major)	Loose fringed
Lower-Grade Officers (Lieutenant to Captain)	Fringeless

Apparently of little concern to the Ottomans, at the time, Crimean War commentators specifically mention that the Turkish Army rank system did not make sense to British Officers[72]. In the case of the Turkish Contingent set up for the Crimean War, an 1856 British Government Parliamentary Report extract shows the British providing NCO-rank chevrons, for the Infantry and the Artillery Soldiers transferred into the Contingent to help with identifying the various ranks of Junior Officers[73]. It was the case at this time that all the Junior Officer grades - Onbasi: Corporal, Cavus: Sergeant, Bascavus: Sergeant-Major, all used an identical insignia consisting of large red tape inverted 'V' shapes on the sides of the tunic collar.

OFFICER'S TUNIC

The 1861 Era Army Officer's uniform (for the Infantry, Artillery and Cavalry) followed the same basic design, as had been in the Crimean War Period. Only Soldiers were given Zouave uniforms. It consisted of a dark blue long skirted tunic with low collar and a single row of seven gilt buttons. The skirt length stopped just above the knees. There were no rear pocket flaps, except for a rear vent ending in two rear-waist buttons. Crimean War Period Officer tunics had a great deal of variety in the collar colour, cuff design, and trim. To accommodate the new cuff rank insignia the cuffs were universally changed to pointed versions. The 1861 Era Officer's tunic was a universal pattern with red collars and cuffs, and line of red tape that went down the front buttons, terminating at the hemline. Dark blue trousers and black shoes completed the dress. Gold epaulette bridles were fitted to the shoulders, and Crimean War Period versions were still used. Typically, the epaulettes were only fitted for ceremonial roles.

Officers were also distinguished, wearing a gold brocade belt with two inner red lines, separated by a narrow gold tape mounted on a red Morocco leather backing. The buckle was identical to the Soldier's version. It was broadly square with cut-off corners, displaying an upwards pointing crescent badge. As it was a higher quality, a frame-border was added to the buckle face. An open framed slightly oval buckle, was also provided on the wearer's right-side to allow it to be adjusted to the waist-size. The belt was provided with sword-hook, on its left side, to suspend the sword scabbard ring from. In addition to this there was a scabbard ring sling that looped onto the belt.

A variation of the Officer's tunic is known that displayed some fashion elements common in the 1860s European and United States Armies. The skirt rather than cut strait from the waist distinctly bellowed-out, and the fabric was gathered along the waistline making the skirt fabric form into deep pleats. The Officer's tunic could have a Zouave cuff. This was a button edged back cuff-slit running up to the elbow. This appears as a band of wide tape edging the base of the cuff, and running along

---

72 Norman, 1985.
73 War Department, 1856.

the back-seam edges, one side of which is edged with a line of buttons, that in some versions are left permanently open, and in other versions have a corresponding row of cord loops, to close the sleeve around the cuff.

TURKISH ARMY OFFICER'S RANK INSIGNIA 1861

▲ Two illustrations from a larger 1900s German chart for the Turkish Army shows the General Staff collar insignia, likely dating to the 1861 Era, and Officer's 1861 Era tunic cuff chevrons[74].

---

74 Ruhl, 1900.

1861 OFFICER'S RANK INSIGNIA

Evidence for the 1861 Era rank system is somewhat fragmentary. A set of 1907 illustrations shows Officers from the 1860 till 1876 Period[75], depicting use of gold, silver (or a combination of both) cuff chevrons to show their rank. The following list of Officer's ranks uses older known phonic spellings of Ottoman terms[76]. These ranks were identified with the following cuff chevrons arrangements:

Miralai	Colonel	Four gold tape cuff chevrons
Kaimakam [Kaymakam]	Lieutenant-Colonel	Four: one gold, one silver, one gold, one silver alternating tape cuff chevrons
Kolagasi	Adjutant-Major	Three gold tape cuff chevrons
Bimbashi	Major	Two (one gold/one silver) tape cuff chevrons
Yuzbashi	Captain	Two gold tape cuff chevrons
Mulazim-i-Evvel	Full-Lieutenant	One gold tape cuff chevron
Alay Katipleri	Regimental Secretary	Three silver tape cuff chevrons
Tabur Katipleri	Battalion Secretary	Two silver tape cuff chevrons
Mulazim-i-Sani	Lieutenant	One silver tape cuff chevron

1861-1876 JUNIOR OFFICERS RANK INSIGNIA

The 1861 Era Junior Officer's sleeve and cuff designs are known from several 1907 dated illustrations[77]. A surviving 1861 Era Turkish Army Zouave jacket in a museum collection has red tape chevrons added to each pointed cuff[78]. Red indicated either the Infantry, Cavalry, or Artillery. Green indicated the Chasseur A'Pied. Yellow distinguished the 1st Imperial Guard Infantry Regiment. A set of one, two or three cuff chevrons were used to show rank.

Onbasi: Corporal	One cuff chevron
Cavus: Sergeant	Two cuff chevrons
Bascavus: Sergeant-Major	Three cuff chevrons

In the case of the Bascavus: Sergeant-Major three more variations are known, using: (1) Pointed trefoil knots; (2) Pair of full-sleeve double trefoil knots; or, (3) Done in cord-work. These possibly related to the Cavalry and Artillery:

Cavalry	Bascavus: Sergeant-Major	Three cuff chevrons	Top cuff chevron end with an extended pointed trefoil knot
Artillery	Bascavus: Sergeant-Major	Three cuff chevrons	Top cuff chevron ends with full-sleeve double trefoil knots
Artillery	Bascavus: Sergeant-Major	Three cuff chevrons	Top cuff chevron ends with cord-work trefoil knots

Toward 1876, the Junior Officer's rank insignia began to simplify and transition from cuff-ranks to sleeve rank badges (one to four large red or gold chevrons worn clipped with hooks on the right arm only). The Bascavus: Sergeant-Major's rank changed with the addition of a last-most forth gold chevron (the other three remained red). This occurred with the insertion of a new lower-grade Junior Officer, called a Bascavus Muavini: Assistant Sergeant-Major (identified with three sleeve chevrons). After 1876, this changed to four red chevrons. The Artillery develop higher technical grades (above the Bascavus), namely a Topcu Cephene Bascavus: Artillery Armourer Sergeant-Major, with two red and two gold sleeve chevrons (1876 till 1908 Artillery).

---

75 Sevket, 1907.
76 Roubicek, 1978.
77 Sevket, 1907.
78 Askeri Muze, 2017.

1861 ARMY GENERALS' UNIFORMS AND RANK INSIGNIA

The 1861 Senior Officers - Mousheer [Mushir]: Marshal, Feriq [Ferik]: General de Division, and Mir-el-Liwa [Liwa]: General de Brigade were largely identifiable with two different rank systems – both were variations of the basic system of cuff chevrons. A set of Court Uniform illustrations are known, and possibly date to early-1861, and relate to the final year of Sultan Abdulmecid. The illustration shows a Feriq [Ferik]: General de Division wearing a blue tunic, with heavily gold embroidered red collar, and two wide heavy gilt tape cuff chevrons over red pointed cuffs. Heavy gold epaulettes, light blue trousers with broad gold side stripes and black shoes complete the dress.

An 1895 dated painting shows a Crimean War Period Pasha: General[79][80]. The uniform was worn as a generic Court Dress. This was a heavily gold embroidered frock coat with laurel garlands, and floral work covering the collar, round cuffs, chest, down the front of the skirt, around the lower hemline, and up the back vent terminating in more floral work around the back. Heavy gold epaulettes, white trousers with broad gold side stripes and black shoes completed the dress. The 1861 Era version of this uniform had become more standardized, and simplified. Known from a 1907 illustration of the Grande Tenue: full dress Mir-el-Liwa [Liwa]: General de Brigade[81]. This shows a blue tunic with heavily gold embroidered lapels. The skirts are plain. French sleeve knots – a pointed set of trefoil knots continuing up the forearm from the top chevrons above the cuff were arranged in the following way:

Mousheer [Mushir]	Marshal	Four woven gilt tapes
Feriq [Ferik]	General de Division	Three woven gilt tapes
Mir-el-Liwa [Liwa]	General de Brigade	Two woven gilt tapes

Heavy gold epaulettes, dark blue trousers with broad gold side stripes and black shoes completed the dress for an 1861 Era General.

Rank insignia could appear as a small set of tape-work covering only the forearm. The same insignia could also be large-embroidered and tape-work, or cord-work covering nearly the entire sleeve, ending just under the epaulette fringe. By the 1870s, for Gala Occasions a detachable heavily gold embroidered cloth cover for the pointed cuffs was introduced.

1861 GENERAL STAFF COLLAR INSIGNIA

The Army General Staff, did not occurred till well after 1837[82]. The first mention of a General Staff, between 1861 and 1876, is the General Staff School, a three-year course following graduation from the military schools. The collar insignia largely relates to 1869, where further military reorganization led to, "a Prussian-like General Staff ... established under the Ministry of War."[83] The red collar displayed a heavily gold embroidered globe of the Earth, map measuring calipers, Officer's sword under a crescent, followed by trophy of flags, and weapons[84].

REGIMENTAL AND BATTALION SECRETARY

The ranks of Alay Katipleri: Regimental Secretary, and Tabur Katipleri: Battalion Secretary[85], were added after the 1843, and 1848 Turkish Army Organization Laws[86]. The uniform is possibly represented in an 1907 illustration, misidentified as an Officer d'Artillerie: Artillery Officer, and dated to the Era of Sultan Abdulmecid[87]. This Officer wears a dark blue tunic, with dark blue collar (with red

---

79 Anatole, 1895.
80 Roubicek, 1978.
81 Sevket, 1907.
82 Roubicek, 1978.
83 Yildiz, 2012.
84 Ruhl, 1900.
85 Askeri Muze, 1986.
86 Roubicek, 1978.
87 Sevket, 1907.

tape edge) and pointed dark blue cuffs topped with two silver cuff rank chevrons. This combination suggests a Tabur Katipleri: Battalion Secretary, as the Artillery typically had red facings till 1861. After 1876, the Secretary rank was identified with two silver lines on a cuff-flap. The Alay Katipleri: Regimental Secretary was identified with three silver cuff rank chevrons. The uniform collar, and tunic front display a red tape edge. Dark blue trousers and black shoes complete the uniform.

POST-1876 USE

As stated, the cuff rank chevrons system continued in use after 1876, and was used till 1908[88]. The cuff chevrons also developed into a series of French-styled sleeve trefoil knots using gold cord-work, tape (for higher grade Officers), and thick tape for Generals. The rank system continued to be used through-out the 1878 till 1908 Era for all Officer's uniforms where a pointed cuff was used. Some of these uniforms, like the Dragoon's Court Uniform[89], by 1908, had been used since the 1861 Era, and still retained cuff chevrons, alongside later-1876 rank systems. By 1900, this rank system was used by Gendarmery Officers[90].

▲ Later-1870s Yuzbashi: Captain's French sleeve knot details for a Zouave-style tunic. Followed by a Miralai: Colonel, Mir-el-Liwa [Liwa]: General de Brigade, and Mousheer [Mushir]: Marshal.

---

88 Askeri Muze, 1986.
89 Sevket, 1907.
90 Turker, 2022.

FIGURE 14: Feriq [Ferik]: General de Division (early-1861).

FIGURE 15: Feriq [Ferik]: General de Division's cuff details (early-1861).

FIGURE 16: Feriq [Ferik]: General de Division (1861 Era).

FIGURE 17: Chasseur A'Pied Yuzbashi: Captain.

FIGURE 18: Alay Katipleri: Regimental Secretary's tunic cuff rank chevrons.

FIGURE 18a: Tabur Katipleri: Battalion Secretary' tunic cuff rank chevrons.

FIGURE 19: Officer's brocade belt.

FIGURE 20: General Staff Officer's collar insignia.

FIGURE 21: Miralai: Colonel's tunic cuff rank chevrons.

FIGURE 21a: Kaimakam [Kaymakam]: Lieutenant-Colonel's tunic cuff rank chevrons.

FIGURE 21b: Bimbashi: Major's tunic cuff rank chevrons.

FIGURE 21c: Yuzbashi: Captain's tunic cuff rank chevrons.

FIGURE 21d: Mulazim-i-Evvel: Full-Lieutenant's tunic cuff rank chevron.

FIGURE 21e: Mulazim-i-Sani: Lieutenant's tunic cuff rank chevron.

FIGURE 22: Zouave jacket Infantry Onbasi: Corporal.

FIGURE 23: Zouave jacket Infantry Cavus: Sergeant's cuff rank chevrons.

FIGURE 24: Zouave jacket Infantry Bascavus: Sergeant-Major's cuff rank chevrons.

FIGURE 25: Zouave jacket Bascavus: Sergeant-Major's cuff rank, with pointed trefoil knot. Shown here on an Infantry uniform cuff, but possibly for the Artillery.

FIGURE 26: Zouave jacket Bascavus: Sergeant-Major's cuff rank, with a top chevron formed into full-sleeve double trefoil knots. Shown here on an Infantry uniform cuff, but possibly for the Cavalry.

FIGURE 26a: Zouave jacket for an Artillery Bascavus: Sergeant-Major's cuff rank, with a top chevron formed into trefoil knots using cord-work.

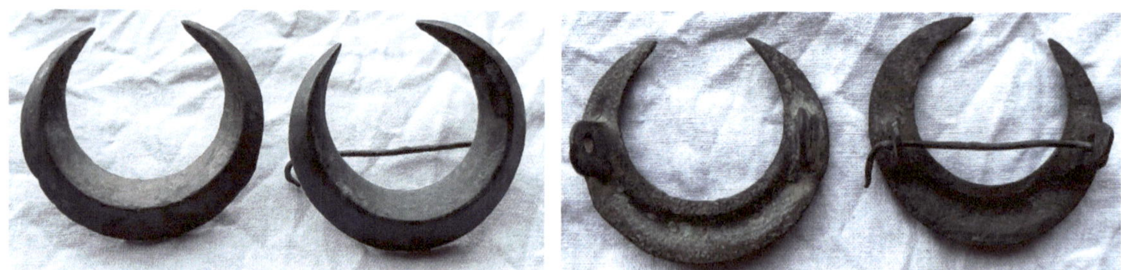

▲ Two examples of smaller cast brass crescent badges of the type commonly used on headdress and equipment insignia by the Army from 1861. Badges of these type did not change in design or manufacture till WW1. Both badges are around 46 millimetres across, and 41 millimetres high.

C.Flaherty
14
15
16
17
18
a
19
20
21
a
b
c
d
e

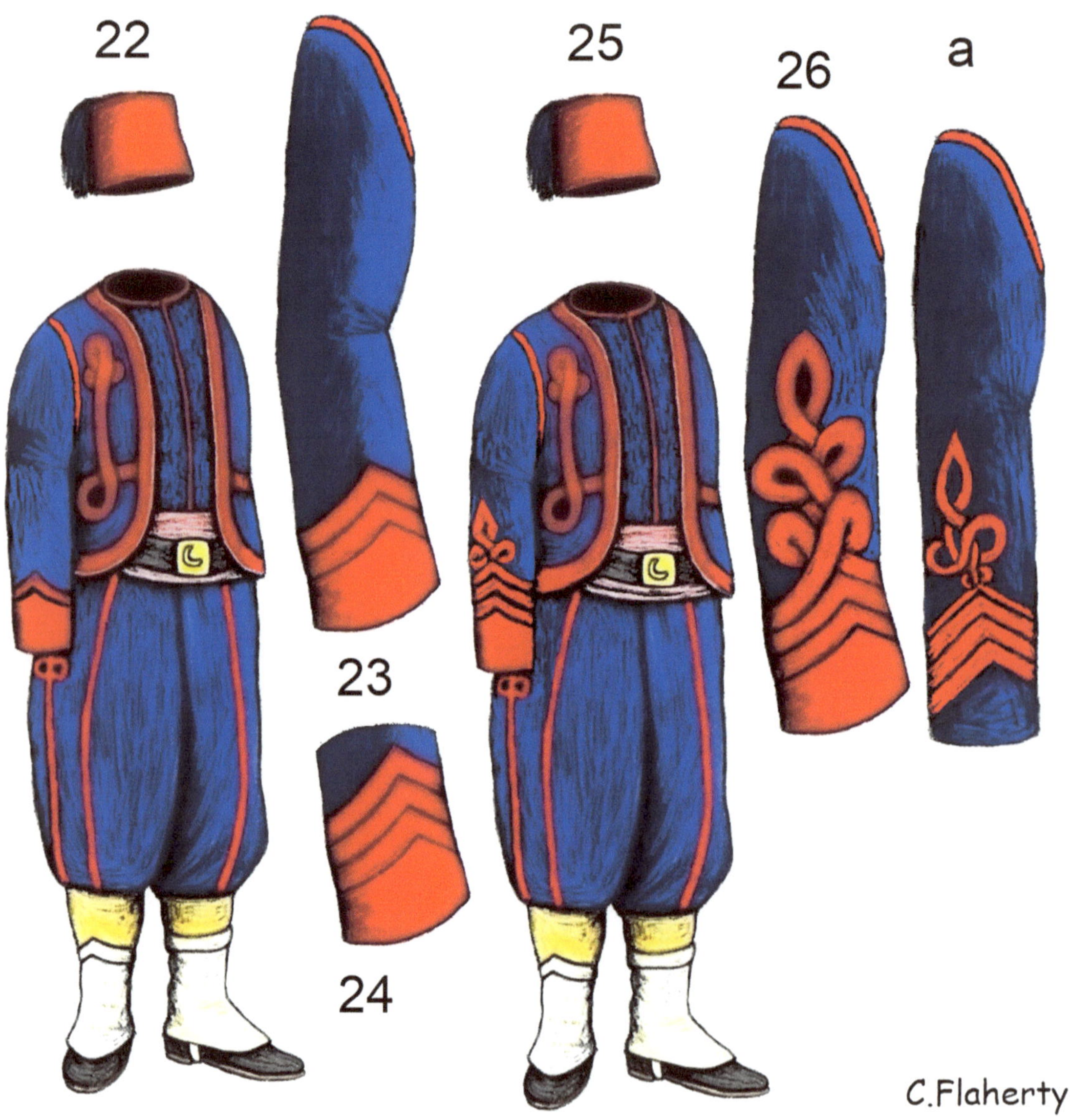
22
25
26
a
23
24
C.Flaherty

CHAPTER 3: PERSONAL EQUIPMENT AND MUSKETS

INTRODUCTION

"The import of American arms that started during the period of Sultan Abdulaziz did not continue due to the failure of the Ottoman administration to find funds. Approximately 600,000 rifles with different characteristics were purchased from American producers such as Enfield, Springfield, Snider, Martini-Henry, Winchester and Remington."[91]

The 1861 Era, saw the widespread standardization of the Army Soldier's basic equipment than had been seen during the Crimean War Period, which was a mix of outdated Napoleonic Period designs[92], and more up to date Soldier's equipment sourced from France, with the large-scale importing of percussion rifled muskets, which replaced the basic flintlock most Turkish Infantry were equipped with.

SOLDIERS BACKPACK

In the Crimean War Period, the Turkish Army bought from France 80,000 Soldier's backpacks[93]. A 1907 illustration of the 1861 Era backpack showed it remained a square version, with a black finish, with two white carry straps[94]. The back flap of the pack came down to the base and had two shorter side pieces (coming half-way down the sides). These were attached to the top, inside part of the back-flap. Straps were attached to the top of the flap to secure a rolled blanket, pray rug (Turkish Soldiers always carried), or the greatcoat. The water bottle was stowed on the back of the backpack and was secured by a cross-strap that buckled around the pack to secure it.

RUSSIAN IRON WATER BOTTLE

The Crimean War Period water bottle, according to commentators was a large iron Russian type, which was slung at the rear of the pack[95]. The 1861 Era version is shown in a 1907 illustration[96]. The bottle appears smaller than the Russian type used previously, and had an oval shaped top and base, with a tall wide funnel and cap. It was secured to the backpack with a harness incorporating a partial cover with a hole for the funnel to pass through and a strap went centrally down the face of the bottle passing through the cross-ways securing strap on the backpack. The harness strap appears to have passed under the water bottle's base and connected at its back.

WAIST BELT, AMMUNITION POUCH AND FROG

Crimean War commentators noted Turkish troops had been equipped with black belts of the latest French pattern with a plain brass square buckle[97]. The French belt equipment sets are assumed to have been the Model 1845, which had a cartridge pouch looped onto the back of the belt. This contained a compartment for caps. The basic change to occur in the 1861 Era was modifying the belts to take a Turkish copy of the basic French plain brass square buckle, adding to the face an upwards pointing crescent badge. The Turkish version of the French waist belt buckle was broadly square with its corners cut-off, and in some cases had a deep recessed edge.

The waist belt was used to support a single ammunition pouch, such as the German 1874 Model Patronentasche fur Infantry, it and similar types of pouches are known to have been used and copied

---

91 Karakoc, 2020.
92 Norman, 1985.
93 Cetin, 2016.
94 Sevket, 1907.
95 Norman, 1985.
96 Sevket, 1907.
97 Norman, 1985.

in the Ottoman Empire. A 1907 illustration shows the ammunition pouch as having back-loops (to fit it onto the belt), and has a heavy short flap, that only covers the top half of the pouch. It is shown with side panels to help cover the opening at the top. It had a closure strap attached to the flap buttoning onto its base[98]. Other ammunition pouches – such as the French Model 1845, or Turkish copies of this version with full face covering flaps, were also used carrying a cast brass crescent badge. The bayonet frog, was made from heavy leather, and was a generic-type used for a number of long sword-sabre bayonets, imported with their percussion rifle muskets, with belt-loop, and hole in its face allowing a scabbard button to pass-through.

FIREARMS

In the Crimean War Period, the basic Infantry Soldier's firearm was described as a French Napoleonic Era flintlock[99]. It is known that from 1847, the Army had started to convert to using percussion smoothbores, called Nizam Tufegi: Regulars' Muskets[100]. The Seshaneci: Foot Chasseur Battalions, from 1852, were armed with muzzle-loading rifles called: Seshane Tufegi. In May 1854, the first 2,000 rifled muskets were bought from France, and were the Minie 1851, with sword-sabre bayonets[101]. From 1853, Belgium machine tools were installed at a new small arms factory in the Zeytinburnu district of Constantinople[102]. The factory produced percussion smoothbores till 1857. The Turkish Army also bought from France, some 40,000 percussion smoothbores, including munitions, these were delivered by May 1854[103]. By 1854, a large number of British percussion muskets had also been sent to the Turkish Army, as part of the setup of the Turkish Contingent[104].

1863 Purchases

The 1861 Era sees a decade transition to the cartridge breech-loader, which was bought about by a rapid weapons modernization programme initiated in 1863[105]. The Ottoman Empire bought from a consortium of Birmingham gunsmiths: Birmingham Small Arms Limited, an order of 50,000 muzzle-loading Enfield rifled muskets. This was followed by a second order in 1865, for 21,000 Enfield rifles fitted with breech-loading Sinder mechanism, along with this another 6,000 of the Sinder mechanism alone for later conversions. In July 1868, a further order for 3,500 more rifles was made with the Birmingham consortium.

1869 Purchases

In 1869, it is also known, that more weapons arrived via trade with the United States, which sold huge stocks of Civil War Northern and Southern Armies war surplus[106]. It is estimated that some, 114,000 English Enfield rifles, and 125,000 U.S. Springfields were purchased. All these weapons including English Pattern 1860 Short Rifles, and the Post Civil War U.S. Springfield Model 1861, and Model 1863 Rifles were converted to the Sinder breech-loading system at the Tophane: Imperial Armoury in Constantinople.

1870 Till 1871 Purchases

From 1870, and 1871 respectively there were purchases from the Winchester Repeating Arms Company of some 48,314 Model 1866 Repeating Rifles, and 18,425 Carbines[107]. The Winchester Carbines were largely intended for the Dragoon Regiments. In 1872, Sultan Abdulaziz received from the Ismail, Khedive of Egypt some 50,000 Martini-Henry Rifles. This led to a competition, that by 1874, the Aynah Martini: Peabody-Martini Rifle was introduced into Ottoman military service.

---

98 Sevket, 1907.
99 Norman, 1985.
100 Zengin, 2015.
101 Zengin, 2015.
102 Zengin, 2015.
103 Cetin, 2016.
104 Cetin, 2016.
105 Bennett, 2018.
106 Bennett, 2018.
107 Bennett, 2018.

C.Flaherty

▲ The 1861 Turkish Soldier's water bottle, backpack and Russian iron water bottle, belt set and standard buckle.

► A large solid cast brass long-horn crescent badge (6.7 centimetres across, and 6.2 centimetres high). A large version like this, was used on cartridge pouches.

▶ The 1861 Turkish Army buckle is depicted in illustrations and photographs as broadly square with cut-off corners, displaying an upwards pointing crescent badge. This set of star and crescent buckles (upwards pointing) shows some other versions commonly used in the 1860s and 1870s.

Some higher quality buckles had a frame-border added to the buckle face. Officer's buckles were carried on gold and red striped brocade belts. Soldiers wore either black or white leather belts.

FIRST - The brass version of the star and crescent buckle is broadly rectangular and measures approximately 50x60 millimetres. The Turkish Army largely adopted the French Army Soldiers' le Ceinturon: Belt Model 1873, this was a standard 52 millimetres wide belt. This implies a local produced version were also made. The slightly reduced belt width – under 50 millimetres, would have still accommodated the back-loops of the ammunition pouch, such as the German 1874 Model Patronentasche fur Infantry: cartridge pouches known to have been used and copied in the Ottoman Empire.

SECOND – A variation cast in steel alloy also measures approximately 50x60 millimetres.

THIRD - Based on the French 1873 model buckle, an 1876 Turkish Army buckle. Based on earlier models used from the 1860s. It displayed a side-ways facing crescent badge. This square cast brass buckle measures 60x60 millimetres, taking a 52 millimetres wide belt, based on the French le Ceinturon: Belt Model 1873.

CHAPTER 4: SULTAN'S STANDARD, SANJAKDAR: STANDARD BEARER AND IMAM DU REGIMENT

INTRODUCTION

A universal pattern banner, was awarded to each Army Regiment, between 1843, and 1844, by Sultan Abdulmecid, in order to bring his newly organized Army closer to European styled Regiments, each with its own standard[108]. Called, the Sultan's Standard it was carried by a dedicated Officer, traditionally called a Sanjakdar: Standard Bearer Officer, but the actual rank was a Lieutenant, or a Sergeant carrying a Company flag.

THE SULTAN'S STANDARD

The 1844 Sultan's Standard given to all Army Regiments (Infantry, Cavalry or Artillery), is thought to have been a high quality red banner that displayed a silver crescent badge, in silver, on a red field[109]. In the 1861 Era, there is a strong possibility that the early Ottoman Government National Flag was also used, with a multi, or six pointed star (which was common in the period), added to the crescent. Banners were carried on a black wood pole and were topped with a gilt crescent finial. Over the same period the banner's leather bandoleer was covered with red cloth, and edged with gold tape.

A variety of coat of arms had appeared during various early reigns. One well known version is from the Sultan Abdulaziz Period and was a ship's aftercastle decoration appearing as a Baroque shield bearing the Tugra, with a display of crossed flags with crescent finials, trumpets, cannon, spears and other weapons[110]. It was only in 1882, that new standards were given to the Army Regiments by Sultan Abdulhamid that incorporated an actual state coat of arms.

▲ The later 1882 till 1908 Sultan Abdulhamid Standard used by Army Regiments.

108 Hacisalihoglu, 2007.
109 Deroy, 1855.
110 Imperial Dockyards, 1861.

SANJAKDAR: STANDARD BEARER

The 1843 Turkish Army Organization Laws saw the rank of Sanjakdar: Standard Bearer Officer abolished[111]. However, each Battalion or Regiment still had an Officer dedicated to carrying the unit flag. The Sanjakdar: Standard Bearer Officer, was personally responsible for the Sultan's Standard and usually commanded an attending squad of two to five soldiers. The Sanjakdar rank was identified in the 1861 Era wearing an Officer's uniform, and appears to have ranked as a Mulazim-i-Sani: Lieutenant. A Flag Cavus: Sergeant at the Company level were also known. The Sanjakdar Officer was distinguished around the 1870s wearing an Officer's tunic decorated with black tape breast lines with each tunic button. The detail is still seen in the 1890s showing a Sanjakdar Officer[112]. An 1890 dated illustration of Ottoman Army Soldiers during the 1877 Russo-Turkish War, also shows the decoration used by an Army Staff Officer, or Headquarters' Rider accompanying an Army General[113]. Appearing as six, or seven Hussar-styled cords ending in loops, with each tunic button.

IMAM DU REGIMENT

Introduced in the 1860s, newly appointed Imam du Regiment: Regimental Imam, to each Army Regiment are depicted wearing a green turban, which was known to denote, "a man who has religious privileges"[114]. The Imam du Regiment are also depicted wearing a long black flowing gown with long wide sleeves[115]. Replacing the Officer's tunics and dress swords Battalion Imams were wearing from 1853[116], and through-out the Crimean War Period. It is possible, by the late-1870s a rank system based on cuff chevrons was introduced, as this was seen later, after 1876. Ranks were established distinguishing a Regimental (three silver tape cuff chevrons), and Battalion Imams (two silver tape cuff chevron)[117]. A Regimental Mufti had the top chevron in gold. After 1876, red collars and cuffs are shown added to the gowns[118]. All Navy ships had an Imam as part of the Company. After 1876, the Navy Imam were shown distinguished with green on their cuffs[119].

▲ Seen after 1876, an Army Regimental Imam (three silver tape cuff chevrons), with red cuffs. A Ship's Company Imam (two silver tape cuff chevrons), with a green cuff line.

---

111 Roubicek, 1978.
112 Unknown, 1896.
113 Ollier, 1890.
114 War Office, 2008.
115 Demoulin, 1897.
116 Urquhart, 1852.
117 Askeri Muze, 1986.
118 Askeri Muze, 1986.
119 Askeri Muze, 1986.

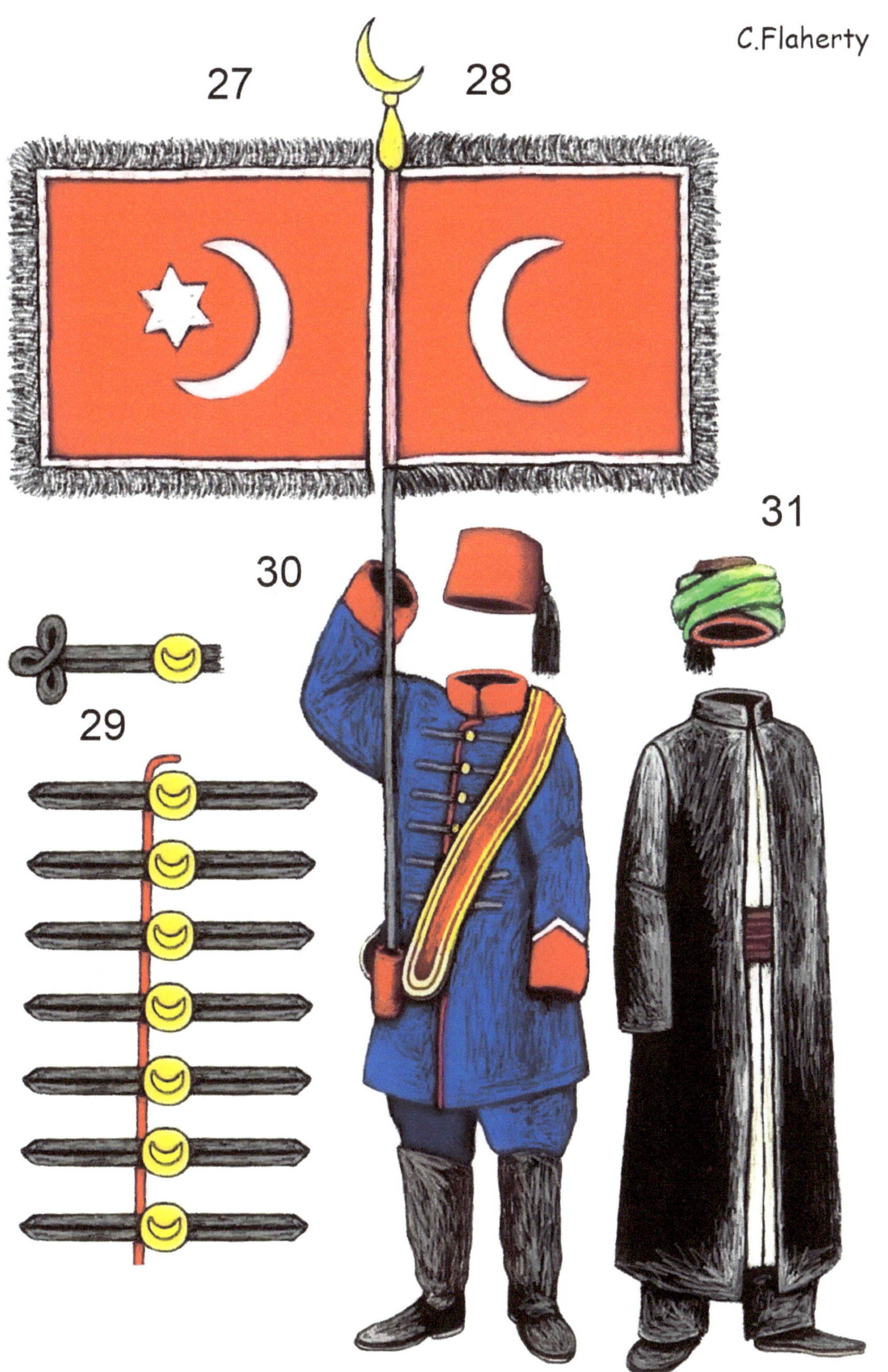

C.Flaherty
27
28
31
30
29

Pag. 39 - FIGURE 27: 1860s Era Ottoman Government National Flag (six point star variation).
FIGURE 28: 1844 Sultan's Standard for an Army Infantry, Cavalry or Artillery Regiment.
FIGURE 29: Sanjakdar: Standard Bearer's tunic chest tape. Early and later versions.
FIGURE 30: Sanjakdar: Standard Bearer Officer.
FIGURE 31: Imam du Regiment.
FIGURE 32: Garde du Palais Halberdier.
FIGURE 33: Garde du Palais Officer's Fez.
FIGURE 34: Gendarmery.
FIGURE 35: Court Security Officer's Ferahi: Gorget.
FIGURE 36: Court Security Officer's cuff details.
FIGURE 37: Court Security Officer.

CHAPTER 5: GENDARMERY, GARDE DU PALAIS AND COURT SECURITY OFFICERS

INTRODUCTION

The Ottoman Court traditionally created a number of policing, and security formations that played a role in Court life, or the operations of the Army. The 1861 Era saw continued existence of the Imperial Court's Halberdiers: known by their title in French from a period illustration as the Garde du Palais, creation of eight new Gendarmery Regiments, and ever present Court Security Officers, who were distinguished from the 18th Century by their Ferahi: Gorgets[120].

GARDE DU PALAIS

A pair of figures from early-1861, which possibly relate to the final year of Sultan Abdulmecid reign identify a Soldier in the Garde du Palais (the Company title in French)[121], and a Chef des Gardes du Palais: Chief of the Imperial Palace Guard Company[122]. After 1876, they became known as the Imperial Courts Halberdiers (a unit commonly featured in most European courts at the time). In the Ottoman Empire's military system, prior to 1826 they were Janissary called the Baltadjis [Baltadjis; Baltaci]: Axeman, Woodcutter, Pioneer, or Halberdier, these had been a Janissary Orta: Regiment whose role (armed with axes) was to clear the Sultan's path of trees on campaign, and to set up his tent. The Axemen traditionally were used to remove obstacles from the path of the Army: clearing trees, levelling roads, and filling swamps. The Axemen also gave its name to a special guard company in the Sultan's Palace: "[They] … were a sort of Lictors who headed the procession when the Sultan appeared in state"[123].

The 1861 Garde du Palais uniform used in Sultan Abdulaziz Court was likely seen at the opening of the Beylerbey [Beylerbeyi] Palace in 1865. The uniform colour had been changed from red, used by the Company during the reign of Sultan Abdulmecid, to a blue tunic, with red pointed cuffs and collar. Much simpler from its previous uniform, which was heavily gold embroidered, the only indication of any special status was the display of several gold tape chest bars. The new headgear was different from the previous one used. It was now a large Busby with a gilt metal front plate displaying a large star over an upwards pointing crescent badge. An upright white and black horsehair plume with a rosette badge was mounted on the front. Light blue trousers with broad gold side stripes and black shoes completed the dress.

The Chef des Gardes du Palais: Chief of the Imperial Palace Guard Company uniform was a more elaborate version of the Soldiers. The Chief ranked as a Feriq [Ferik]: General de Division. Distinguished with a heavily gold embroidered collar, and chest bars, and wide heavy gilt tape cuff chevrons. Heavy gold epaulettes, light blue trousers with broad gold side stripes and black shoes completed the dress. The Fez had a similar set of badges and plume to that used by the Soldiers in the Company.

GENDARMERY REGIMENTS

Between 1861, and 1876, eight Gendarmery Regiments were created. The Regiments were known by their geographical titles[124]:

---

120 Eruretin, 2001.
121 Unknown, 1850.
122 Unknown, 1850.
123 Blackwood, 1841.
124 Roubicek, 1978.

HISTORICAL TITLE	MODERN DAY LOCATIONS	
Brousse Gendarmery Regiment	Bursa	North-Western Anatolia (Turkey)
Smyrne Gendarmery Regiment	Izmir	Province Capital Western Extremity of Anatolia
Angora Gendarmery Regiment	Ankara	Central Anatolia
Kastamonia Gendarmery Regiment		Capital District of Kastamonu Province (Turkey)
Konia Gendarmery Regiment	Iconium	City in South-Central Turkey
Trebizond Gendarmery Regiment		Black Sea Coast City North-East Turkey
Hedjaz Gendarmery Regiment		Region in the West of Saudi Arabia
Yemen Gendarmery Regiment		South Arabia

As a new formation the Gendarmery were uniformed in the Zouave uniform. An illustration of a Soldier and Officer pair, misdated to 1896 as the Soldier is shown armed with a musket, and misidentified as Infantry[125], shows light-blue jackets with yellow facings, blue pants tucked into high white leggings with black shoes. The Gendarmery uniform distinctions were:

GENDARMERY	Jacket	Cuffs	Tape	Pocket	Pants	Special Distinctions
All Regiments	Light Blue	Light Blue	Yellow	Red	Light Blue	Red Waist Band

The Gendarmery Officer is depicted wearing a plain dark blue double breasted tunic, with six rows of gilt buttons, with plain dark blue collar and pointed cuffs. Gold cuff chevrons – the top one ending with a pointed trefoil indicated the rank. Dark blue trousers with narrow red side stripes and black shoes complete the uniform.

COURT SECURITY OFFICER

A 1876 illustration of a Court Security Officer[126], shows him wearing a long flowing skirted Zouave-styled single breasted tunic with eight gilt buttons, with button edged back cuff-slits running up to the elbow. The cuffs are plain, and the open collar appears edged in gold tape. Around his neck he wears a Ferahi: Gorget, with a six point star embossed on it (an upwards pointing crescent would also be a possibility). He only has an epaulette bridle on his right shoulder to hold an aiguillettes-shoulder cord. Wide pants were tucked into high boots, to complete the dress.

---

125 Unknown, 1896.
126 Unknown, 1876.

CHAPTER 6: CAVALRY

INTRODUCTION

Cavalry was nominally divided into two types of Mounted Soldier: Lancer, or Dragoon. Crimean War Period Cavalry had a distinctly Napoleonic appearance, dressed in Hussar-styled uniforms and using horse equipment like the end-pointed schabracke, with sheepskin cover, and round valise, that were Napoleonic Period relics. The 1861 Era sees a drastic change in uniforms and horse equipment.

ORGANIZATION

The 1861 Era Cavalry Regiment comprised six Squadrons, each of which had 90 Soldiers, in peacetime and 140 in wartime. It doubled its effective number by amalgamating with local Redif: Reserve Cavalry in each Ordu: Army. At this time, a Cavalry Soldier would spend in Regular Service five years in the Nizam: Regulars, then another six years in the Redif: Reserve, and a final eight years in the Saliss [Mustahfız; Moustahfeez]: Territorial Army.

By 1877, at the start of the Russo-Turkish War, the Turkish Army had 186 Cavalry Squadrons. This number included some 50 Volunteer Cavalry Squadrons.

The 1861 Era Cavalry Regiments retained territorial designations, from the Crimean War Period. However, it is not clear if these remained the same or changed later. The Regiments were also still numbered from one to four within their respective Ordu: Armies.

1ST ORDU: ARMY	4TH ORDU: ARMY
1st Lancer Cavalry Regiment Isnik	1st Cavalry Dragoon Regiment Tocat
1st Imperial Guard Cavalry Regiment	2nd Cavalry Dragoon Regiment Van
2nd Imperial Guard Cavalry Regiment Tyra	3rd Cavalry Dragoon Regiment Mardyn
3rd Cavalry Regiment Karahissar	**5TH ORDU: ARMY**
4th Cavalry Regiment Sparta	1st Cavalry Dragoon Regiment Havran
Cossack Brigade	2nd Cavalry Dragoon Regiment Tripoli
2ND ORDU: ARMY	3rd Cavalry Dragoon Regiment Deirulkamar
1st Cavalry Dragoon Regiment Babadagh	4th Cavalry Dragoon Regiment Hama
2nd Cavalry Dragoon Regiment Yuzgad	Camel Corps
3rd Cavalry Dragoon Regiment Angora	**6TH ORDU: ARMY**
4th Cavalry Dragoon Regiment Konia	1st Cavalry Dragoon Regiment
3RD ORDU: ARMY	2nd Cavalry Dragoon Regiment
1st Cavalry Dragoon Regiment Jannina	**7TH ORDU: ARMY**
2nd Cavalry Dragoon Regiment Prezrin	Circassian Squadron
3rd Cavalry Dragoon Regiment Sophia	
4th Chasseurs-a-Cheval Regiment Cherbajiy	

▲ The 1848 Turkish Cavalry Regiments territorial titles (mostly using old spellings) in each of the seven Ordu: Armies[127][128]. By the 1861 Era, the 6th Ordu: Army had lost two of its Cavalry Regiments. It is not known if this was from Baghdad, Bassora, Mossul, Derie and Nejd, or from Jidda.

---

127 Urquhart, 1852.
128 Roubicek, 1978.

1ST LANCER REGIMENT

The 1861 Era 1st Lancer's uniform retained its features from the 1840s which consisted of a blue shell-jacket with red collar, pointed cuffs, and lapels, as a special distinction on the front of the jacket – all edged with white tape; the tape was lost around the 1870s, and white Russian or German button tabs were added to the collar and cuffs[129]. A French model lance was used. The pennant was plain red, with a swallow tail. Some versions may have displayed a white star and crescent. Blue pants with wide red side stripes, and black riding boots completed the dress. The 1st Lancer Officers, were the only ones to wear the same tunic as the rest of the Soldiers in the Regiment. The Officer's uniform was fitted with gold shoulder bridles for wearing their rank epaulettes.

1861 FRENCH ZOUAVE CAVALRY UNIFORMS

A 1907 illustration[130], and 19th Century colourized lithograph[131], are known of the Imperial Guard Cavalry in their red Zouave uniforms. Both depict the uniform for the 1st or 2nd Imperial Guard Cavalry who adopted French Zouave-styled uniforms. The uniform distinctions were as follows:

CAVALRY REGIMENT	Jacket	Cuffs	Tape	Pocket	Pants	Special Distinctions
1st Imperial Guard	Red	Dark Blue	Yellow	Red	Dark Blue	Red Waist Band
2nd Imperial Guard						Yellow Cuff Tape
						Red Cuff Base

The most distinctive feature of the Imperial Guard Cavalry's Zouave uniforms was the addition of a button edged back cuff-slit running up to the elbow. This appears as a band of wide red tape edging the base of the blue cuff, and running along the back-seam edges, one side of which is edged with a line of buttons, that in some versions are left permanently open, and in other versions have a corresponding row of cord loops, to close the sleeve around the cuff.

The 1st Ordu: Army's 3rd and 4th Cavalry Regiments received identical versions of the Zouave uniform:

3rd Cavalry	Dark Blue	Dark Blue	Red	Dark Blue	Dark Blue	Red Waist Band
4th Cavalry						

The 3rd and 4th Cavalry Regiments' uniforms were identical to Infantry ones, and like the Imperial Guard Cavalry, their main distinction was wearing riding boots and carrying Cavalry swords.

COSSACK BRIGADE

After the Crimean War, Officers and Soldiers of the Sultan's Cossack Brigade, went into the 1st Guard Cossack under Michal Czajkowski[132]. The Cossack were given Guard status in 1857, and were shifted from the 3rd to the 1st Ordu: Army. Remaining in Turkish service until its destruction around 1876[133]. After the Crimean War, the disbanded Cossack Division (that had been under English command) became a base forming a new Dragoon Division (which consisted of two Regiments), with the Cossack Regiment (forming the 6th, and 7th Squadrons) under the command of Czajkowski. At the beginning of 1857, Czajkowski and his Regiment were sent to guard the Greek border. In 1862, they were part of the Imperial Guard Divisions. From around 1866, the Cossack Brigade now had four Divisions (8 Squadrons), divided into a Cossack, and Dragoon Regiments. There had been a proposed expansion of the Cossack Brigade into more Regiments; however, this did not eventuate.

---

129 Sevket, 1907.
130 Sevket, 1907.
131 Roubicek, 1978.
132 Czajkowski, 1883.
133 Cliff, 1997.

If this had happened, distinctions would have been as follows (and would have followed the 1861 cuff colours system for the Line Dragoon Cavalry Regiments):

1st Cossack Division	Blue Coat	Red Collar	Red Cuffs
2nd Cossack Division	Blue Coat	Red Collar	White Cuffs
3rd Dragoon Division	Blue Coat	Red Collar	Crimson Cuffs
4th Dragoon Division	Blue Coat	Red Collar	Light Green Cuffs

Unlike the rest of the Turkish Army that wore the Civilian Fez, the Cossack in Ottoman service wore a variety of fur-covered Busby styles. From the 1860s the Cossack uniform underwent changes, and several early photographs exist depicting the Officers. The actual chronology is impossible to identify. The earliest uniform consisted of a loose fitting buttonless frock coat, with double sleeves and was the same as that worn by the Crimean War Period Cossack Brigade. It was the origin for the Dragoon Regiment's tunic, which also had double sleeves. A Busby was worn, with thick, long tassel lines (that buttoned under the left shoulder, under the epaulette). A star and crescent set of badges was worn on the front of the Busby, and pompom on its top side. The next two iterations lost the outside coat sleeve, and a tape line was added to the Busby top. A single breasted tunic with low rounded collar, pointed cuffs, seven or eight gilt buttons appeared next. The headgear consisted of a long cloth cap, with a broad fur brow band. A final version, from the 1870s, appears to have be based on the Chevaulegers' jacket, with a Fez that has been given a broad fur brow band. This displayed a crescent badge, and oval badge showing the Sultan's Tugra. Chin scales were added. The final Officer's headdress type had a lot in common with later Russian Cossack Cavalry examples, consisting of a cloth skull cap with a broad rounded fur brow band, with long tassel lines (that buttoned under the left shoulder, under the epaulette). It appears that Soldiers in the Brigade around 1876 wore a low Busby with a star and crescent badge[134]. The 1870s Chevaulegers' jacket had a double line of breast buttons, but only had red piping along the left side of the lapel edge, which also ran along the hemline. The facings were either red collars, and pointed cuffs piped white[135], or blue collars (edged all round in red tape), blue pointed cuffs (edged top and bottom with red tape) with three cuff seam buttons, and blue shoulder boards with red tape edging[136]. White belts, and carry straps were used. Pouches were white leather with silver plates. Officer's versions had red button-on covers. Blue breeches with red side stripes and riding boots completed the dress.

Around 1854, the Cossack Regiment-Brigade reused an old banner of the Zaporozhian Cossack, which had been kept in Constantinople, following the 1828 Ottoman-Russian war. Originally described as silk, with a cross on a blue background. An account says the Cossack Brigade flag was two-sided, on the front there was the crescent and on the back a cross. This could be referring to a two-halved flag consisting of an Ottoman flag, combined with the old banner of the Zaporozhian Cossack, added on the end, as is often seen in modern illustrations. More likely, the old banner of the Zaporozhian Cossack was incorporated onto the reverse side of a standard Turkish Army flag, such as that later used in 1861, by the 1st Cossack Regiment.

LINE DRAGOONS

The pre-1880 (from around 1861), version of the Dragoon uniform consisted of a double sleeve buttonless (using hooks and eyes, later was buttoned) long skirted blue tunic with a folded-down red collar (that later became standing)[137]. The blue outer sleeve front seam was split, and closed with three groups of three buttons. The red inner sleave had a plain cuff. The tunic had plain red shoulder

134 Unknown, 1896.
135 Unknown.
136 Unknown, 1896.
137 Sevket, 1907.

boards. Blue breeches and riding boots completed the uniform. Line Dragoons provided Cavalry for the 2nd, 3rd, 4th, 5th, and 6th Ordu: Armies. They were organized into Brigades of four Cavalry Regiments each.

▶ The outer sleeve cuff showed the Regiment's facing:	1st Dragoon Cavalry	Red Cuffs
	2nd Dragoon Cavalry	White Cuffs
	3rd Dragoon Cavalry	Crimson Cuffs
	4th Dragoon Cavalry	Light Green Cuffs

The 3rd Ordu: Army's 4th Cavalry Chasseurs-a-Cheval Regiment Cherbajiy[138], prior to the Crimean War developed into a special unit of Chasseurs-a-Cheval: Mounted Rifles Cavalry with a distinctive uniform, that may have had green facings. Under the 1861 Era organization it remained the 4th Dragoon Cavalry Regiment, identified by its green cuffs. After 1878, when consecutive numbers was introduced for the Cavalry, it stayed the 4th Cavalry Regiment with green facings (the rest wore red).

CIRCASSIEN VOLUNTEER CAVALRY SQUADRON

The 1861 Circassien Volunteer Cavalry Squadron uniform are depicted wearing a classical version of the Cossack dress, complete with a large Busby (displaying a large upwards pointing crescent badge), this also had a red cloth flap with yellow lines[139]. Soldiers wore a blue long flowing wrap around frock coat with chest pockets for spare cartridges. A red short, collared shirt was warn under this. The coat and chest pockets were trimmed in red and yellow. Soft brown-yellow boots completed the uniform. Two other illustrations are known of the Circassien Cavalry, while misdated, appear to be from the mid-19th Century, one is titled: "Turkische Cavallerie Tscherkessen [Turkic Cavalry Circassians]"[140][141]. This shows a mounted figure, and horse with a small green schabracke with rounded front end, and pointed back end, with a broad white coloured border. A grey undecorated round valise is retained under the back of a brown leather riding saddle. Another large blanket role appears slung over the horse at the front of the saddle. The figure wears a green Cossack coat with low collar, all with white tape trim. This appears to be an Officer, as wide yellow and white bands are shown above the cuff tape trim. The other Soldier, only has the trim edge. Both figures wear a white cloth tall domed hat, with a large neck curtain. The Circassians served in Yemen, and the unusual headgear may be a type of sun protection. Straight brown pants and black shoes completed the uniform.

KAZAKHSTAN VOLUNTEER CAVALRY

1861 Era Kazakhstan Volunteer Cavalry are known from a 1907 illustration[142]. Shown wearing a low lambswool cap with an upwards pointing crescent badge, with yellow bag and tassel end. The collarless waist jacket is dark blue, as are the pantaloons. Both are covered with heavy gold patterned embroidery. Black riding boots complete the dress.

WAIST BELT AND CARTRIDGE BOX

The 1861 Era Cavalry wore the same waist belt and buckle used by the rest of the Army, with sword slings looped on. The Crimean War Period Cavalry cartridge box (dating from 1848), and its carry strap was used throughout the 1861 Era. The square pouch had sides faced with brass plates, with rings mounted, for the carry strap to hook onto. The square ended front flap was edged with a brass stripe, and the flap displayed an upwards facing crescent badge. The front end of the carry strap had

138 Czajkowski, 1962.
139 Sevket, 1907.
140 Unknown, 1896.
141 Unknown, 1896.
142 Sevket, 1907.

a square, or sometimes heart-shaped plate with a crescent, or star and crescent badge. Behind this a metal arrow lock-pick on a chain could be inserted. The arrow lock-pick chain was connected to a crescent badge mounted further up.

▲ An example of the carry strap plate for the 1st Lancer Regiment.

HORSE EQUIPMENT

Transition of the horse equipment over the 1861 Era is not well understood, or documented. Items such as the horse bridle, and other equipment was either from the pre-Crimean War Period, or was imported from Europe afterwards, and sometime after, it changed from black to brown leather only. By the 1870s, a clearer picture emerges. Cavalry were equipped with a small dark blue schabracke with both ends rounded. This had a broad red coloured border, that often has a second inner line of red tape, separated by a thin highlight of dark blue cloth showing. A large red cloth angled sideways facing crescent was added to the rear rounded end. A blue cloth cylindrical valise, or portemanteau: saddle case, displays a red end ring, with an inner blue circular patch. The main feature was the use of two large, rounded oblong shaped brown leather saddle wallets, with a broad covered flap closed with a strap and buckle, which were slung over the front of the brown leather riding saddle on either side. Prior to the adoption of saddle wallets it is possible Turkish Cavalry had started to use this area for a large grey blanket roll. Older brace of pistol holsters covered by a sheepskin cover were finally abandoned in the 1860s. New model pistol holster, and rifle buckets was strapped forward of the saddle.

FIGURE 38: 1st Lancer Cavalry Regiment.

FIGURE 39: Cavalry pouch and carry strap back details.

FIGURE 40: Cavalry pouch and carry strap front plate, and lock-pick details.

FIGURE 41: Cavalry pouch with crescent badge.

FIGURE 42: 1st or 2nd Imperial Guard Cavalry Regiment's cuff, and its back details.

FIGURE 43: 1st or 2nd Imperial Guard Cavalry Regiment.

FIGURE 44: 3rd Cavalry Regiment (1st Ordu: Army), and cuff details for a Cavalry Bascavus: Sergeant-Major's cuff rank chevrons.

FIGURE 45: 4th Cavalry Regiment (1st Ordu: Army).

FIGURE 46: Dragoon shoulder board for all Regiments.

FIGURE 47: 1st Dragoon Cavalry Regiment's distinctive outer sleeve cuff colour.

FIGURE 47a: 2nd Dragoon Cavalry Regiment's distinctive outer sleeve cuff colour.

FIGURE 47b: 3rd Dragoon Cavalry Regiment's distinctive outer sleeve cuff colour.

FIGURE 47c: 4th Dragoon Cavalry Regiment's distinctive outer sleeve cuff colour.

FIGURE 48: Dragoon's double sleeve details, showing the front seam split, closed with three groups of three buttons, and red inner sleave plain cuff.

FIGURE 49: 4th Dragoon Soldier (1876).

FIGURE 50: 3rd Dragoon Soldier, with heart-shaped carry strap plate (1861).

FIGURE 51: 2nd Dragoon Officer (1861).

FIGURE 52: Cossack Brigade Officer, and white leather carry strap with pouch details (1861).

FIGURE 53: Cossack Brigade Officer (later-1861).

FIGURE 54: Cossack Brigade Officer (later-1861 variation).

FIGURE 55: Cossack Brigade Busby oval badge displaying the Sultan's Tugra. A multipoint star and crescent badge was also used.

FIGURE 56: Cossack Brigade Officer (later-1861 variation).

FIGURE 57: Cossack Brigade Soldier (1876).

FIGURE 58: Cossack Brigade Soldier's cuff details (1876).

FIGURE 59: Cossack Brigade Officer's cuff details (1876).

FIGURE 60: Cuff colour for the 2nd Cossack Regiment that was never raised.

FIGURE 60a: Cuff colour for the 3rd Cossack Regiment that was never raised.

FIGURE 60b: Cuff colour for the 4th Dragoons that would have been brigaded with the Cossack Regiments (that was never raised).

FIGURE 61: Cossack Brigade Officer (1876).

FIGURE 62: Cossack Regiment-Brigade's flag.

FIGURE 63: Circassien Volunteer Cavalry Squadron, and horse schabracke.

FIGURE 64: Circassien Volunteer Cavalry Squadron cuff details.

FIGURE 65: Circassien Volunteer Cavalry Squadron Officer, possibly in Yemen.

FIGURE 66: Kazakhstan Cavalry.

C.Flaherty
38
39
40
41
42
43

C.Flaherty
44
45

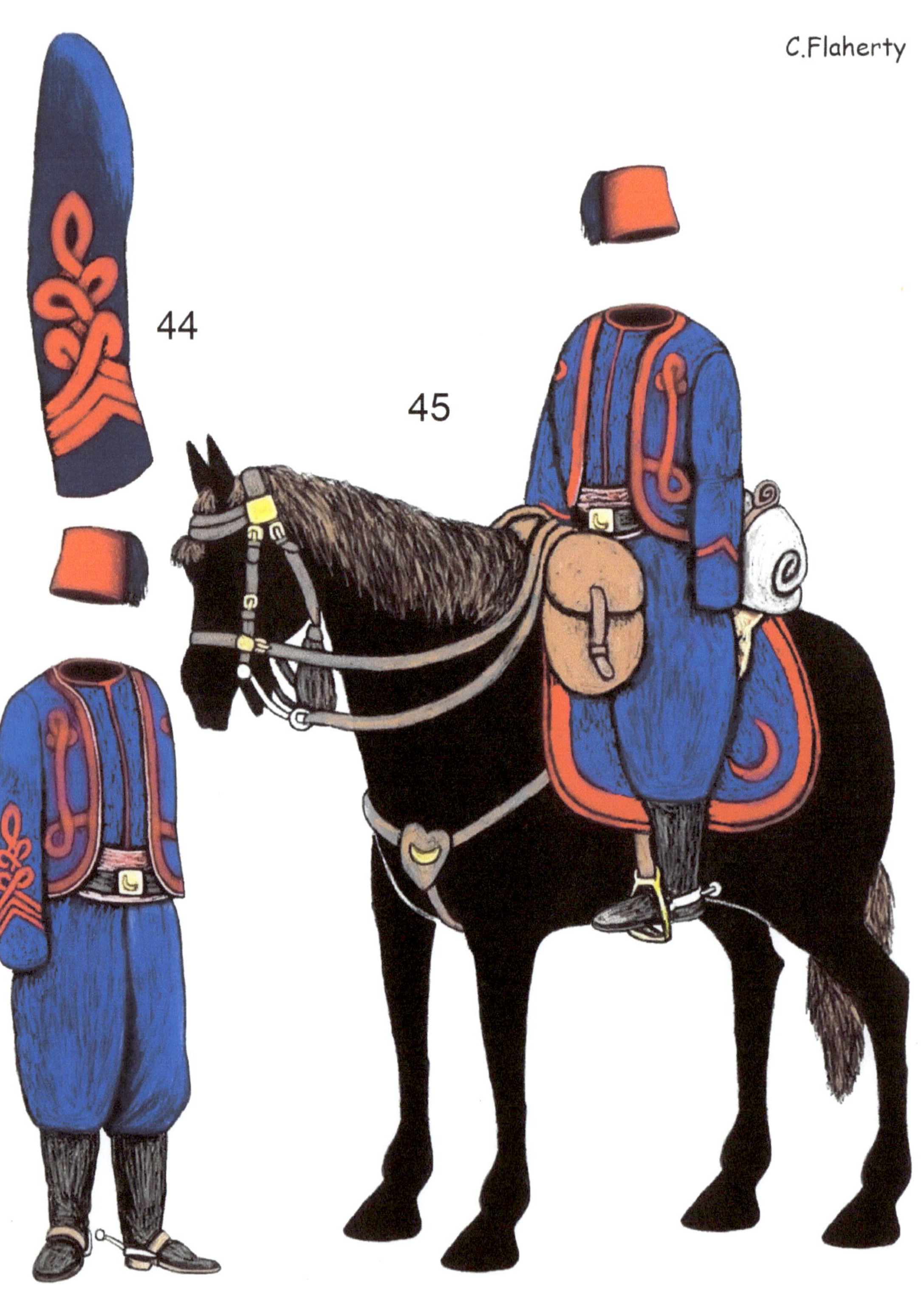

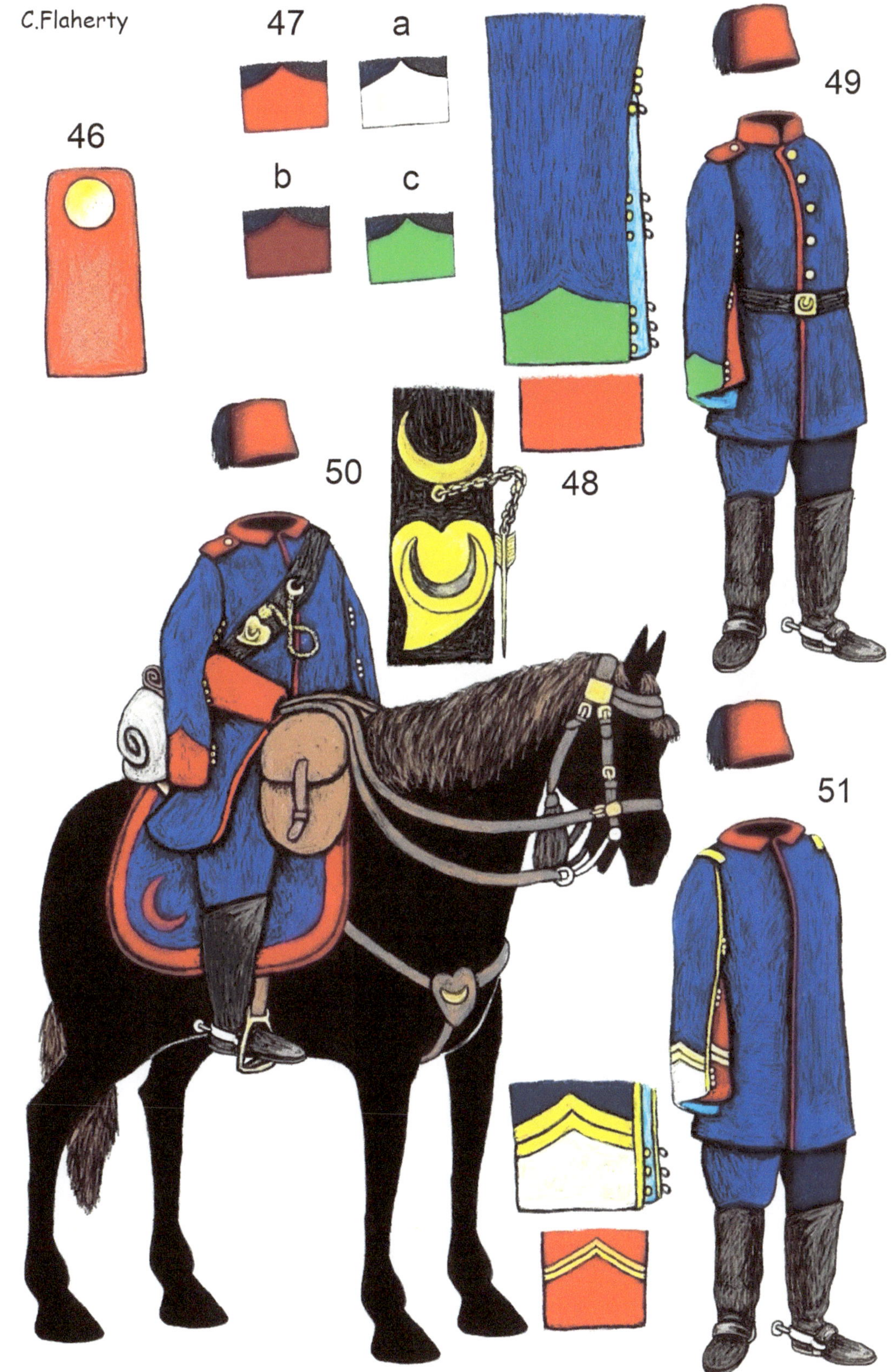
C.Flaherty
46
47
a
b
c
48
49
50
51

C.Flaherty
52
53
54
55
56

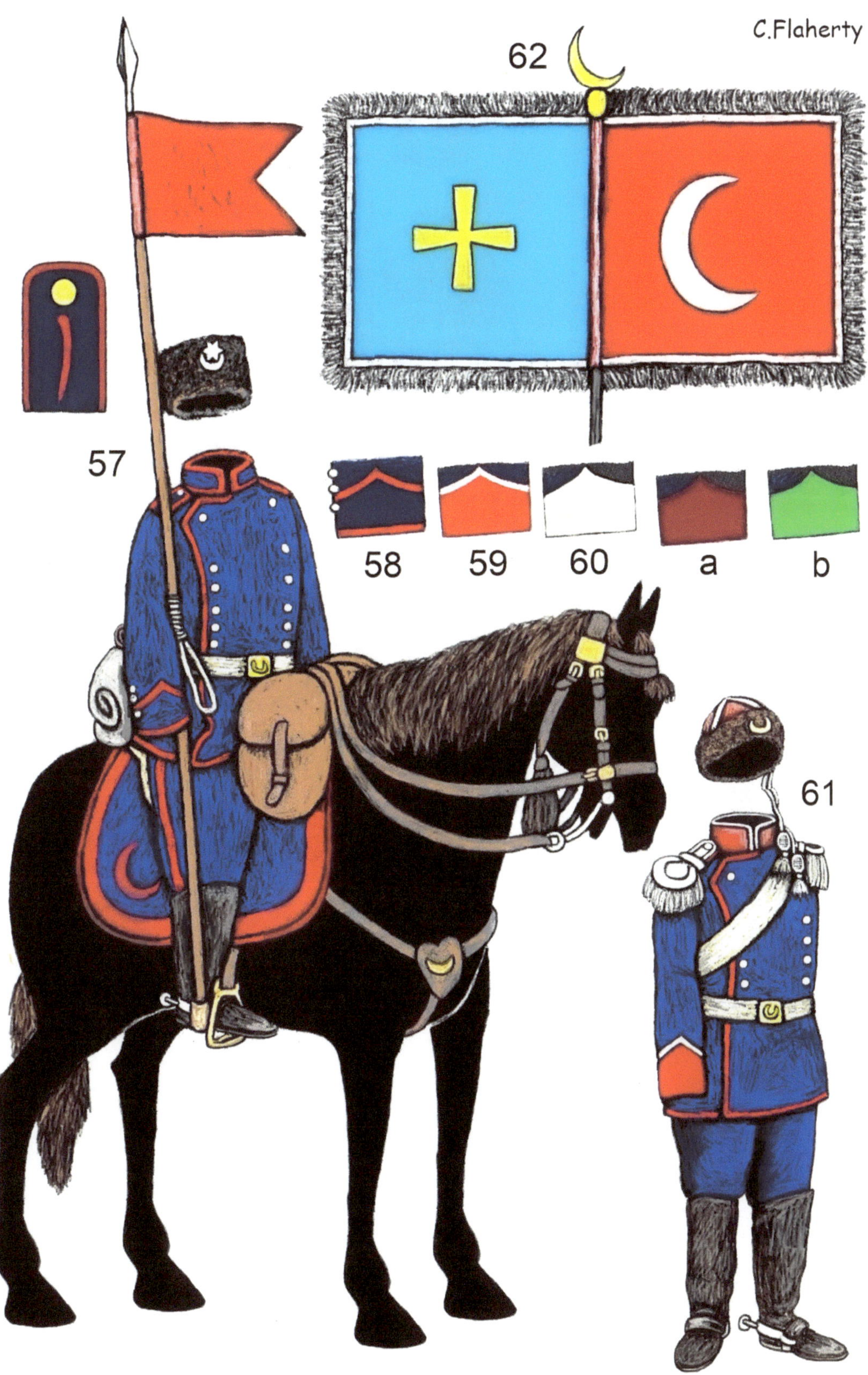
C.Flaherty
62
57
58
59
60
a
b
61

C.Flaherty
63
64
65
66

CHAPTER 7: ARTILLERY

INTRODUCTION

An Artillery Regiment comprised four Battalions of three Batteries each, and each Battery was equipped with six guns. Sultan Abdulaziz, it is said:

> "[had a] … fascination with the technical aspects of his Army enabled Ottoman military purchasing agents to acquire and import thousands of new weapons and a variety of new equipment"[143].

The Krupp Company had previously established a monopoly position in Ottoman Field Artillery[144]. The business had begun around 1861, when Krupp sent a sample gun to Sultan Abdulaziz[145][146]. By 1875, the Ottoman Empire had bought 1,816 Krupp cannon of various calibres[147]. However, a lower figure of 1,486 is also given[148].

The 1861 Era had seven Artillery Regiments – one allotted to each Ordu: Army[149]. That represented around 490 pieces of field ordnance, as each Ordu Artillery Regiment was equipped with around 70 cannon (bronze muzzle loaders) or guns (steel rifled breech-loaders). Around the early-1870s, most of the older bronze muzzle-loading field cannon would have been replaced with the newer Krupp Field Guns, even though much heavier classes of fortress and siege cannon remained in service. Krupp was continuously improving and upgrading its designs with new Artillery technology. Newer models replaced Ordu Artillery Regiment's armaments. The first Krupp sample order was made in 1861, this was its steel barrel, rifled breech loader cannon[150]. This was likely, the 6-Pounder: 6-Pfunder-Feldkanone C/61 (that was also first adopted into Prussian military service).

Newer model Krupp Field Guns, were introduced in 1864, 1867, and 1871, and likely included the following types used in the Turkish Army:

- **6-Pounder: 6-Pfunder-Feldkanone C/64**

- **4-Pounder: 4-Pfunder-Feldkanone C/64**

- **4-Pounder: 4-Pfunder-Feldkanone C/67 (last in that series)**

- **8-Centimetre Stahlkanone C/64**

- **9-Centimetre Stahlkanone mit Kolbenverschluss (1871)**

YEAR	NUMBER BOUGHT
1861	1
1863	48
1864	60
1868	127
1870	88
1871	127
1873	834
1875	201
TOTAL	1,486

It has been stated, that in the Crimean War, the Turkish Artillery, "Batteries may have mixed muzzle-loaders, breech-loaders, smooth-bores and rifled guns in a polyglot fashion"[151][152]. However, this statement may have more relevance to the post-1861 situation, and related to the transition from bronze muzzle-loading cannon rated according to Ottoman Cap: weights, which indicated the weight of the projectile fired by the gun in okka: an Ottoman mass-weight measurement: that ap-

143 Uyar, 2009.
144 Yorulmaz, 2014.
145 Yorulmaz, 2014.
146 Karakoc, 2020.
147 Yorulmaz, 2014.
148 Karakoc, 2020.
149 Roubicek, 1978.
150 Karakoc, E. 2020.
151 Robinson, 1988.
152 Cox, 1997.

proximated 1.29 kg (per okka). The effect on Turkish Artillery organization was it transitioned from the Crimean War Period establishment, through 1861 till 1876, where a Line Regiment of Artillery comprised nine Field and three Horse Batteries[153]. This possibly had 72 Krupp Field Guns (as each of the 12 Batteries, had six guns each), ranging from 4-pounder, 6-pounder, and later 8-centimetre field guns.

ARTILLERY TACTICAL USE

In 1837, the Sultan issued Artillery use regulations that placed, "[a] … greater … [tactical] … emphasis on the use of howitzers … [was made] … mainly due to their light weight."[154] Emphasis on howitzer use gave greater tactical advantages, such as being able to deliver indirect fire. The Crimean War Period emphasis on the howitzer as the main means of battlefield Artillery fire-support had by 1859, in most European Armies changed to new long-range tactics brought about by the transition to gun-howitzers, and then rifled field guns. Firing cylindrical projectiles these carried at a greater range, and could create many of the same effects (such as firing over low walls) that had previously been performed by the shorter range smoothbore field howitzers at a sharply curved trajectory.

HORSE ARTILLERY ZOUAVE UNIFORMS

In the 1861 Era, in order to speed Battery mobility, Gunners were provided with horse mounts, which allowed for a continuing distinction between Field Artillery Batteries, and more mobile ones – still retaining the title of Horse Artillery, or Flying Columns (as these were often known). Nevertheless, Horse Artillery references, in the 1861 Era, is somewhat of a misnomer as by the 1850s, most European Armies had begun to abolish the old distinction between Mounted, Field and Positional Batteries as the rifled field gun revolution saw introduction of limber-caisson wagons with seating for the Gunners, and Gunners riding on horse teams.

Two pictures of the 1861 Era Horse Artillery in their Zouave uniforms are known: A 1907 illustration identified as a, "Soldat d'Artilerie"[155]; and, a 19th Century colourized lithograph, misidentified as an, "Ottoman Gendarme of the late-19th Century."[156] Both show the same figure, an Artillery Bascavus: Sergeant-Major. The Horse Artillery Bascavus: Sergeant-Major wears a high quality French Zouave-styled uniform, with elaborate Arabesque braid, applique, embroidery and tape decoration, and light blue pockets (the coloured space inside the breast looped tape decorations). The three cuff-rank chevrons are topped with an extra-line of lace forming a pointed trefoil knot. This and the other detailing, such as extra lace edging, is of a type and pattern seen used in French Zouave Infantry Non-Commissioned Officer's uniforms in Algeria (Army of North Africa). As the 1861 Field Artillery was a new formation created with the introduction of the Krupp Guns, these were also universally dressed in Zouave uniforms with the following distinctions:

ARTILLERY	Jacket	Cuffs	Tape	Pocket	Pants	Special Distinctions
FIELD ARTILLERY	Dark	Dark	Red	Light	Dark	Red Shoulder Piping
HORSE ARTILLERY	Blue	Blue		Blue	Blue	Red Waist Band

Horse Artillery's only distinguishing feature from the rest of the Field Artillery was wearing riding boots, and carrying Cavalry swords and pouches. The rest of the Artillery followed the Infantry wearing yellow wool stockings, and black shoes covered by white calf spats.

153 Roubicek, 1978.
154 Sakul, 2011.
155 Sevket, 1907.
156 Roubicek, 1978.

MITRAILLEUSES BATTERIES (PAGET GATLING GUNS)

Gatling Guns, built by E. Paget of Vienna, for Halil Pasha, Grand Master of Artillery, were introduced:

> "In late spring ... [1870, when] ... the agent, L.W.Broadwell, travelled to Constantinople and arranged demonstrations for Halil Pasha ... [and] ... negotiated a contract to sell two hundred Gatling Guns, to be manufactured under contract in Vienna, to the Turkish forces"[157].

The swivels were bolted to the gun frame, and could be mounted on static mounts, or transferred to a field carriage. Turkish-Paget Gatling Gun field carriages were based on the Austro-Hungarian Army's version.

It is also known, as part of the Paget order, "the Ottomans brought in outside expertise, former Soldiers from the United States on the Gatling Guns' use"[158]. In 1876, there were 8 Field Artillery Regiments (one of which was a Reserve Regiment based in Constantinople), and a further 7 Garrison Artillery Regiments. Each Regiment was allotted an additional Battery of Gatling Guns (comprising 6 Gatling Guns each). By 1877, an Artillery Regiment comprised: 4 Battalions (3 Batteries each); one Mountain Battery; and six-gun Mitrailleuses Battery[159].

C.Flaherty

▶ An 1873 illustration of the Austrian 'Gatling Szorloveg 1865.M'[160].

▲ Turkish heavy bronze muzzle-loading cannon on its fortress carriage.

---

157 Chivers, 2013.
158 Murray, 2013.
159 Roubicek, 1978.
160 Bulyovszky, 1873.

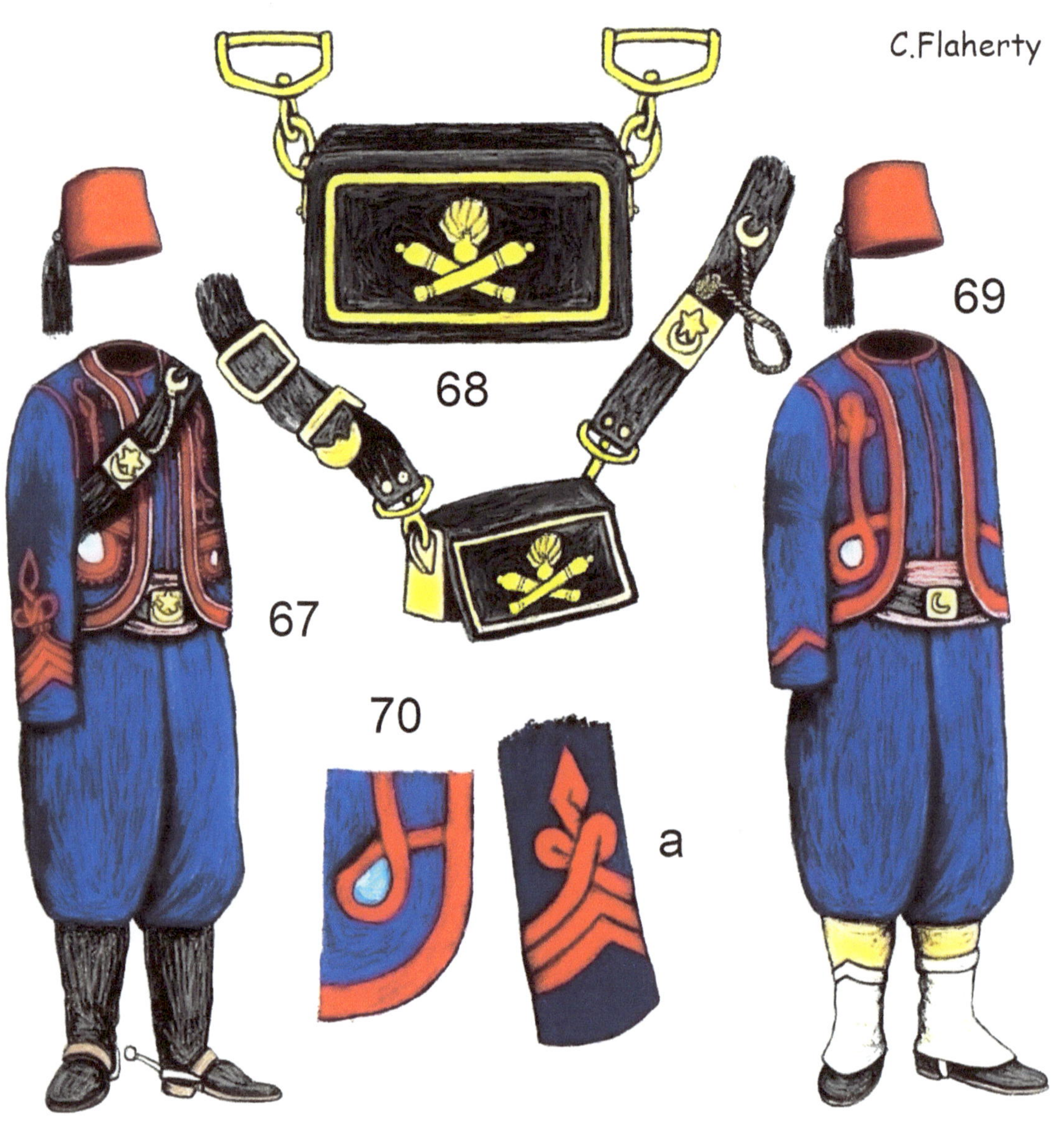

FIGURE 67: Horse Artillery Bascavus: Sergeant-Major.
FIGURE 68: Horse Artillery pouch and carry strap.
FIGURE 69: Field Artillery.
FIGURE 70: Artillery pocket details.
FIGURE 70a: Artillery Bascavus: Sergeant-Major's cuff details.

CHAPTER 8: ALBANIANS

INTRODUCTION

In Egypt, the use of Albanian troops dated as early as 1848, organized as Bashi-Bazouks, they were heavily armed, using: "state-of-the-art weaponry in the form of American revolvers … [presumably the 1848, or 1850 Samuel Colt]"[161]. The Khedive in Egypt, placed great value on the Albanian mercenaries, and by the start of the Crimean War some 4,500 Albanians were part of the Egyptian Army in their traditional role as skirmishers, mountain warfare experts, police, security and body-guard units[162]. In the 1861 Era, seven veteran Albanian Battalions were used in the Turkish Army's Montenegrin Campaign of 1863-1864[163]. The Albanians went on to form the core of a Mufreze: Temporary Independent Detachment, titled the Fırka-i-Islahiyye. This fought in the Province of Kozan (North-East Cilicia), and then the suppression of rebels in Lebanon.

DRESS

An 1859 illustration (misdated to 1820), shows the Albanian Infantry Regiment in Egypt wearing a low collared green jacket with a row of grey metal buttons. The collar has red tape edging, and red piped shoulder seams. The dress included Fustanella: a long-skirted shirt (which later formed part of the Greek national costume). The legs are covered with long green leggings edged in black tape over brown laced-up shoes. The figure wears a Crimean War Period Turkish Army Military Fez. A Balkan Bensilan: a weapons' belt is worn. Crimean War commentators describe Albanians wearing:

> "[a] … jacket of fine red cloth or silk … [with] … braided and buttoned breast … [a] … white many folded … [Fustanella: a long-skirted shirt] … red cap … red gaiters … pointed red shoes … [and] … silken sash"[164].

Another commentator, stated the Albanians, wore:

> "[Albanian dress] … no two had exactly similar costume, but the general character was as follows: A waist-coat made of coloured chintz; a jacket of thick felt, ornamented with devices of black cloth or gold, the sleeves loose as in the case of the Arabs, with inner white linen ones within; a Fez … a white linen petticoat …[Fustanella] … of enormous size, hanging in numberless plaits from the waist to the knee; plain brown or black leather boots, with the tops turned down, the said tops being covered with coloured cloth ornamented to the taste of the wearer"[165].

Albanians were often mounted for transport (they tended to fight on foot), and their:

> "horses of the Albanian Regiments … averaging about thirteen hands high; in fact, the mass were little more than ponies, none larger than cobs."[166]

It is said, of Albanian horse furniture, this had:

> "a metal crescent generally depended from the throat lash instead of a plume, and the reins were coloured ribbon, leather thongs, rope, or even string, according to the fortunes of the owner."[167]

An 1857 painting of the, "Albanians mercenaries in the Ottoman Army" shows for warmth they wore a large heavy goatskin cloak[168]. This illustration shows two figures wearing the Fustanella, with a collarless waist coat with a row of gilt buttons, and gold tape running down the front. A red open sleeved jacket with green lining, and heavy gold tape edging. A small fez with a folded-over top, and long tassel is worn. The legs are bare except for heavily decorated red leggings and red pointed shoes. The Balkan Bensilan: a weapons' belt is also worn.

---

161 Dunn, 2013.
162 Dunn, 2013.
163 Uyar, 2009.
164 Dodd, 1856.
165 Money, 1857.
166 Money, 1857.
167 Money, 1857.
168 Preziosi, 1857.

▲ Albanian mercenaries in the Ottoman Army[169].

169 Preziosi, 1857.

BENSILAN: TRADITIONAL BALKAN WEAPONS BELT

Albanians used the traditional Balkan Bensilan: a weapons' belt. It was described as an immense brown leather appendage fastened round their waists, with receptacles for pistols, dagger, and knife. The Bensilan allowed for the Yatagan curved swords to be carried across the waist. It was further added: "in the majority of cases they had no arms beyond those mentioned … [however] … the pistols were flint, huge and clumsy."[170] Often associated with the Albanian in Ottoman military service, in particular the Navy[171], and the later Imperial Guard Regiment that was formed: 1st Albanian Regiment of the Imperial Guard (1890-1908)[172]. Bronze cap pouches are a typical part of 19th Century Balkan's traditional folk costume. The Albanians also used these.

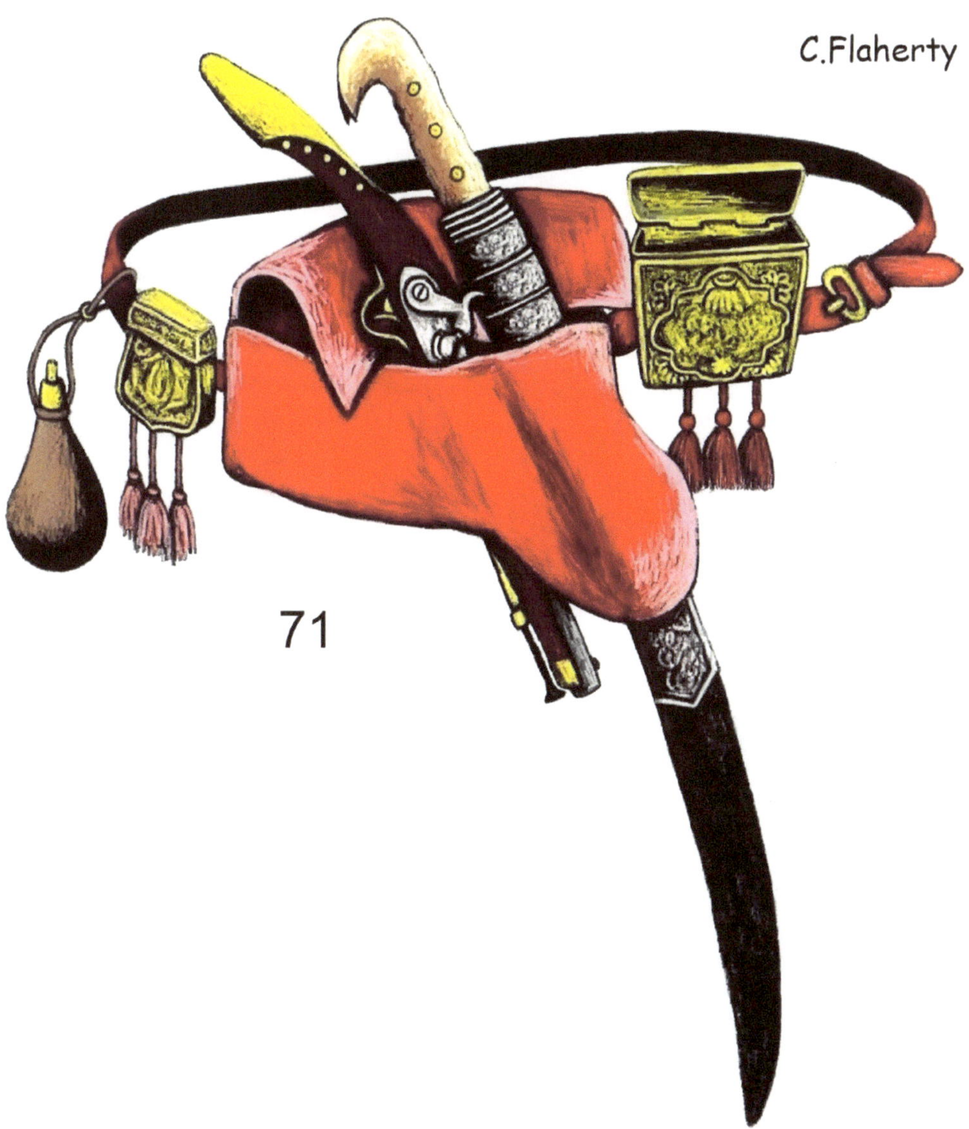

FIGURE 71: Bensilan: Traditional Balkan weapons belt.

170 Money, 1857.
171 Basimevi, 1997.
172 Sevket, 1907.

FIGURE 72: Ottoman Army Albanian Mercenary (1857).

FIGURE 73: Albanian Mercenary in Egypt (1859).

FIGURE 74: Ottoman Army Albanian Mercenary with goatskin cloak (1857).

CHAPTER 9: BASHI-BAZOUKS

INTRODUCTION

By the mid-19th Century, Ottoman military authorities classed Bashi-Bazouks as volunteers to supplement the mobilization of the Nizam: Regular Army on campaign acting as irregular skirmishing troops[173]. They were mustered by Sergerdes: Local Bashi-Bazouks Chiefs. An 1854 observer stated that the term Bashi-Bazouks officially meant, "Irregular Soldier" in the Turkish Army[174]. The Bashi-Bazouks, "or the Asakir-i-Muvazzafa as they were called officially"[175], as an institution was further reinforced by the Sultan, who would call for them to assemble, creating the Bashi-Bazouks fever of 1854[176]. The Sultan regularly declared individuals as Chief of the Bashi-Bazouks, to further coordinate the recruitment and leadership at the start of campaigns. Carrying the Sultan's Firman: Authority, the bearer of which could act in his name, these court-appointed officials would carry Nishans-of-Merit: Military Orders, and Medals, and Berats-of-Rank: Military and Civil Appointments to be given to influential Chieftains, the local Civic Leaders[177]. The carriers of Sultan's Firman often had access to large arsenals, providing weapons, and munitions to the volunteers. Collecting at the Army camps, the Military Administration added names to muster-roles[178]. Integration into local Armies, saw senior-level Civil Leaders, such as Tribal Chiefs put into command positions. The Ottoman military policy using Bashi-Bazouk is understood to have ended during the 1877 Russo-Turkish War, due to their excesses forcing the Ottoman Government to abandon their use[179].

BASHI-BAZOUKS OFFICERS

Two figures from a set of early-1861 Turkish Court uniforms shows two Bashi-Bazouk Officers: one is high-ranking and possibly has the rank of a Feriq [Ferik]: General de Division, and is identified as a Chef des Bachi-Boszouks: Bashi-Bazouk Chief[180]. The Officer figure is identified as an Officier de Bachi-Bouzouks: Bashi-Bazouk Officer[181]. Both uniforms are red double sleeved collarless Bolero jackets over a red collarless waist vest, and are richly edged in gold tape, and embroidery. Around the waist a wide white, red and blue striped wrap or sash is worn. The figures wear tall blue conical hats, with wide white, red and blue striped turbans with fringes hanging loose. Wide blue knee length pantaloons are worn with tight red leggings covered with gold floral embroidery, and red pointed slippers complete the dress.

The Bashi-Bazouks Chief and Officer's uniforms has a number of similarities, to a 1855 illustration identified from the 1820s, "Nizami Djedid Bimbachi Chef de Batailion de la 1st Reform du Sultan Mahmoud [Bashi-Bazouks Chief from the first reforms under Sultan Mahmoud]"[182]. The headgear is near identical to both the Bashi-Bazouks Chief and Officer, except the conical hat appears to be red, rather than blue. The major difference is that the 1855 version shows a sleeved, long skirted gown, worn under a red open sleeved low collared coat with a long skirt. The chest area is covered with thick gold tape and tassels, and the whole coat is richly decorated in gold tape trim and embroidery. Yellow boots complete the dress. In the Crimean War Period accounts mention much the same dress being associated with the Bashi-Bazouks. General Beatson, it is said:

173 Aksan, 2013.
174 Slade, 1867.
175 Badem, 2010.
176 Slade, 1867.
177 Badem, 2010.
178 Badem, 2010.
179 Encyclopædia Britannica.
180 Unknown, 1850.
181 Unknown, 1850.
182 Brindesi, 1855.

Another Crimean War Period Officer - Richard Francis Burton also said,

The early-1861 Era Officier de Bachi-Bouzouks: Bashi-Bazouk Officer, has been depicted in a uniform similar to that of the Chef, with less embroidery and simpler cuff chevrons that look similar to Army versions used at the time. Both uniforms use the Zouave cuff detail, with a button edged back cuff-slit running up to the elbow. This appears as a band of wide tape edging the base of the cuff, and running along the back-seam edges, one side of which is edged with a line of buttons.

The cuffs of the Bashi-Bazouks Chief are decorated with thick gold tape chevrons, ending with what appears to be a crescent badge. After 1876, this insignia was used to identify an Aide-de-Camp to the Sultan[185]. This allowed the wearer to act in the Sultan's name[186]. The Bashi-Bazouk Officer's cuff decoration used narrower gold cuff chevrons. The 1861 Era, saw first attempts creating a uniform, and rank system for the Bashi-Bazouk. It is known, that the Bashi-Bazouk were organized as Cavalry and Infantry Brigades of Companies, under the command of a Chief, with the rank of Bimbashi: Major. Army Officers commanded Companies and Squadrons, with the rank of Yuzbashi: Captain, and Mulazim-i-Evvel: Full-Lieutenant, and these would have used similar uniforms, that may have had the following Officers and Junior Officers' ranks:

Bimbashi: Major	Three gold cuff chevrons
Yuzbashi: Captain	Two gold cuff chevrons
Mulazim-i-Evvel: Full-Lieutenant	One gold cuff chevron
Cavus: Sergeant	Wide wavy tape around the jacket edge and around the sleeves
Onbasi: Corporal	Double tape lines around the jacket edge

In regards to the Junior Officers: Cavus: Sergeant, and Onbasi: Corporal, it was likely the case, these rank's insignia were less formal than the Officers, and were identified by the use of extra gold tape and embroidery on the jackets.

BASHI-BAZOUK OR ZEIBEK INFANTRY SOLDIERS

Two figures from a set of early-1861 Turkish Court uniforms shows Infantry figures, armed with percussion muskets, and wearing black leather French Infantry belts. Described as, "Zeibek"[187]. The two figures wear uniforms with close similarities to the Bashi-Bazouk Chief, and Officer. Both wear a Fustanella: long-skirted shirt of Greek origin, which has been pulled up and wrapped around the waist, and secured by the belt, revealing wide blue knee breeches. These are worn with tight red leggings covered with gold floral embroidery, and blue pointed slippers. The figures wear the same tall blue conical hats, with wide white, red and blue striped turbans with fringes hanging loose. Each figure wears a red Zouave jacket over a blue collarless vest edged in wide white tape. The jackets are edged in gold tape, one with a double-line border, and the other with a thick wavy line border, perhaps indicating different Junior Officer's ranks. The Soldiers are both wearing Army backpacks. A pistol is shown tucked into the cloth above the belt. The Zeibek: Irregular Militia are well known from an 1885 illustration showing a group with their distinctive tall domed headgear wrapped in

---

183 Rice, 2001.
184 Lovell, 1998.
185 Askeri Muze, 1986.
186 Mango, 1999.
187 Unknown, 1896.

fringed shawls[188]. The same headgear appears in an 1869 painting of a Bashi-Bazouks[189]. It was also commonly seen in the Crimean War Period. It was commented about this unique headgear, that:

> "[The Bashi-Bazouks] … so that he does not comply with the modern fashion of the Turks at Constanti-nople, and cover his head merely with a red cap; but he twines an immense shawl in picturesque folds round and round it, till he looks, when sitting down, like a gigantic mushroom"[190].

▲ A Group of Zeibek[191].

188 Zher, 1885.
189 Gerome, 1869.
190 Dodd, 1856.
191 Zher, 1885.

An 1854 illustration, identified as a, "Bachi-Bouzoug"[192], shows a similarly very tall and rounded fez, wrapped with a shawl. The odd appearance of the Bashi-Bazouks headgear and other dress by the standards of the 1861 Era was noted earlier in the Crimean War Period. Commentators, stated: "[they had] … their own fashion … wear bizarre and wild-looking dresses, and are armed with long rifles."[193]

An 1876 illustration of the Barracks of the Bashi-Bazouks at the Chibouk Chular Khan, Adrianople shows plainer unadorned Zouave uniforms (without the use of many layers of shawls), with a Civilian Fez[194]. This suggests the Bashi-Bazouk only tended to dress-up, in their tall hats and wrap shawls around their headgear and body to create a more shocking effect on their opponents.

MOUNTED BASHI-BAZOUK

An 1897 illustration shows a mounted Bashi-Bazouk, dressed in the Zeibek-style[195]. The horse furniture depicted has a medieval appearance. Consisting of a long red cord horse apron, attached to red circular shields depicting a star and crescent badge with laurels. Connected to a green saddle with a high pointed saddle pommel with a brass onion shaped finial. A small red schabracke with rounded front end, and pointed back end, has a wide yellow border; not unlike the regular Turkish Army version used at the time. However, large brass metal Arabian stirrups are used instead of regular ones.

BASHI-BAZOUK FLAG (1855 AND 1876)

Bashi-Bazouk generally carried a large green flag, on a red pole with a silver spear point. This detail can be seen in an 1863 painting[196]. Whereas an 1876 illustration shows a large Ottoman Government National Flag with a crescent and star, and up-pointed gilt metal crescent finial[197].

FIGURE 75: 1855 Bashi-Bazouks Chief.

FIGURE 76: 1861 Bashi-Bazouks Chief.

FIGURE 77: 1861 Bashi-Bazouks Officer.

FIGURE 78: 1861 Bashi-Bazouks Chief's cuff rank chevrons with a crescent badge.

FIGURE 79: Bashi-Bazouks Officer's cuff rank chevrons.

FIGURE 79a: Possible Bashi-Bazouks Yuzbashi: Captain's cuff rank chevrons.

FIGURE 79b: Possible Bashi-Bazouks Mulazim-i-Evvel: Full-Lieutenant's cuff rank chevron.

FIGURE 80: Large Ottoman Government National Flag with multipoint star and crescent.

FIGURE 81: Bashi-Bazouks Flag Bearer.

FIGURE 82: Bashi-Bazouks Cavus: Sergeant.

FIGURE 83: Bashi-Bazouks Onbasi: Corporal.

FIGURE 84: Bashi-Bazouks Ordinary Soldier's barrack's uniform.

FIGURE 85: Bashi-Bazouk Ordinary Soldier's high hat.

FIGURE 86: Bashi-Bazouk Ordinary Soldier.

FIGURE 87: Mounted Bashi-Bazouks Soldier.

FIGURE 88: Mounted Bashi-Bazouk Soldier and saddle details.

192 Raffet, 1854.
193 Koppen, 1890.
194 Illustrated London News, 1876.
195 Boussod, 1897.
196 Vernet, 1860.
197 Illustrated London News, 1876.

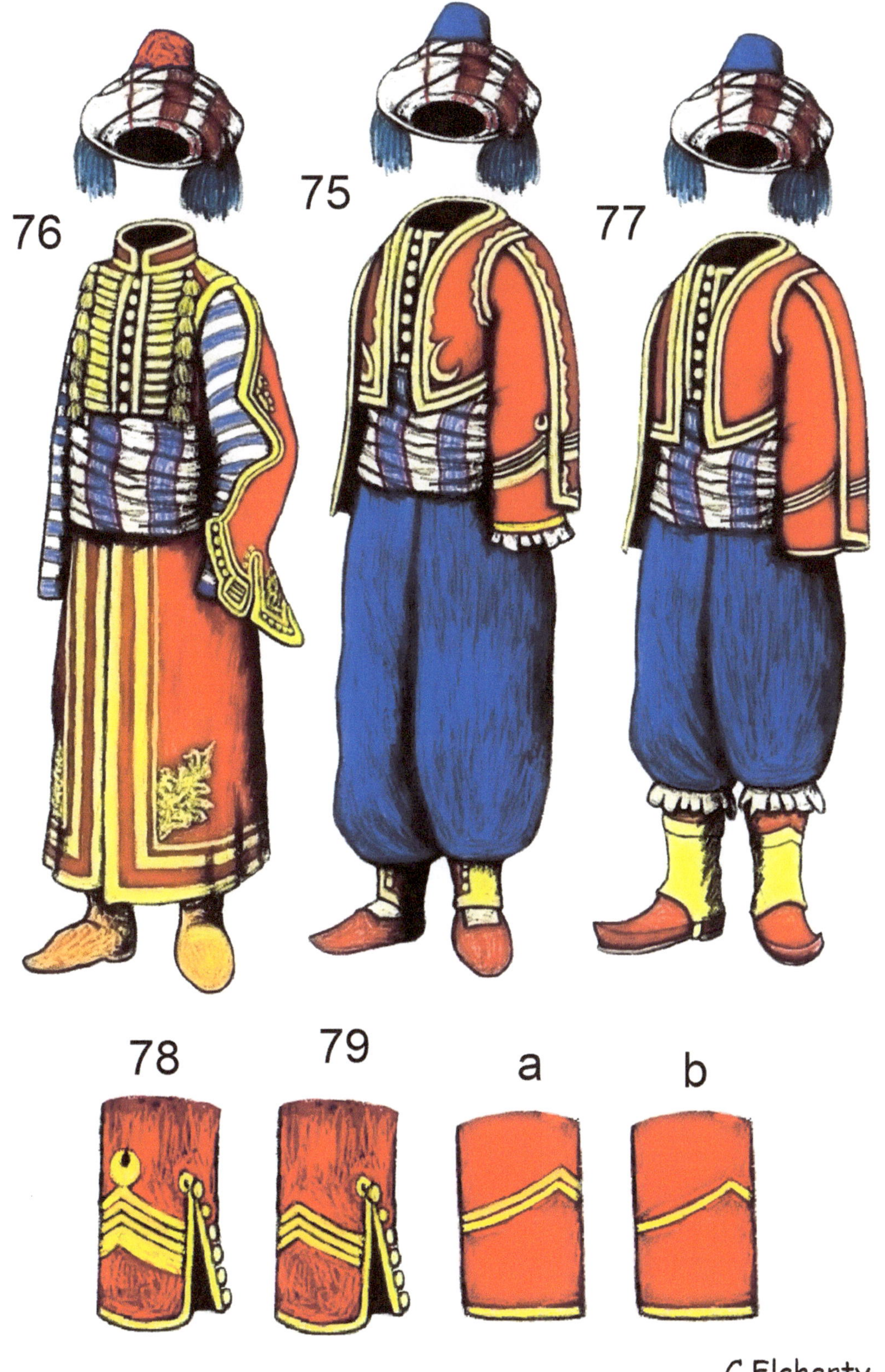

76
75
77
78
79
a
b
C.Flaherty

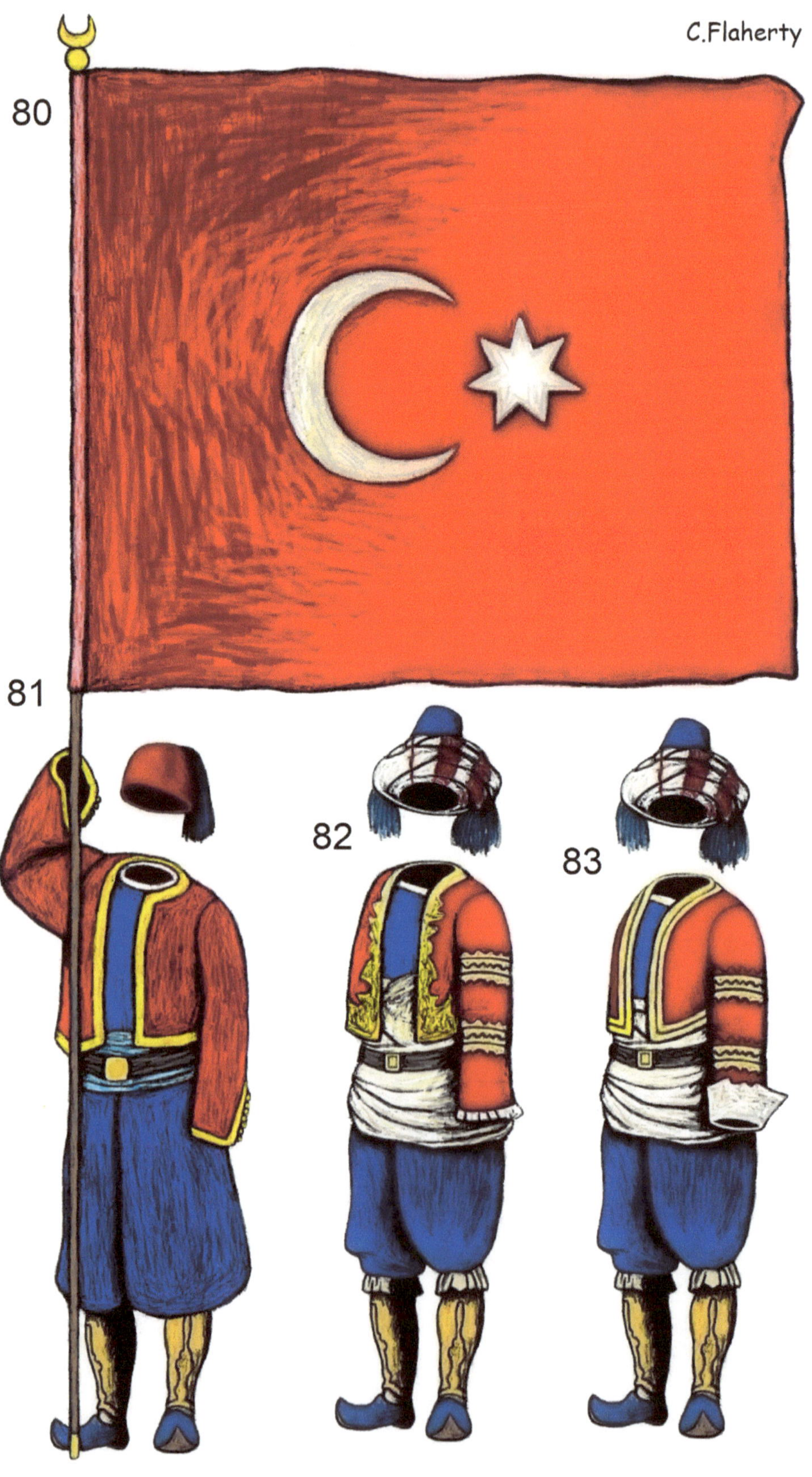

C.Flaherty
80
81
82
83

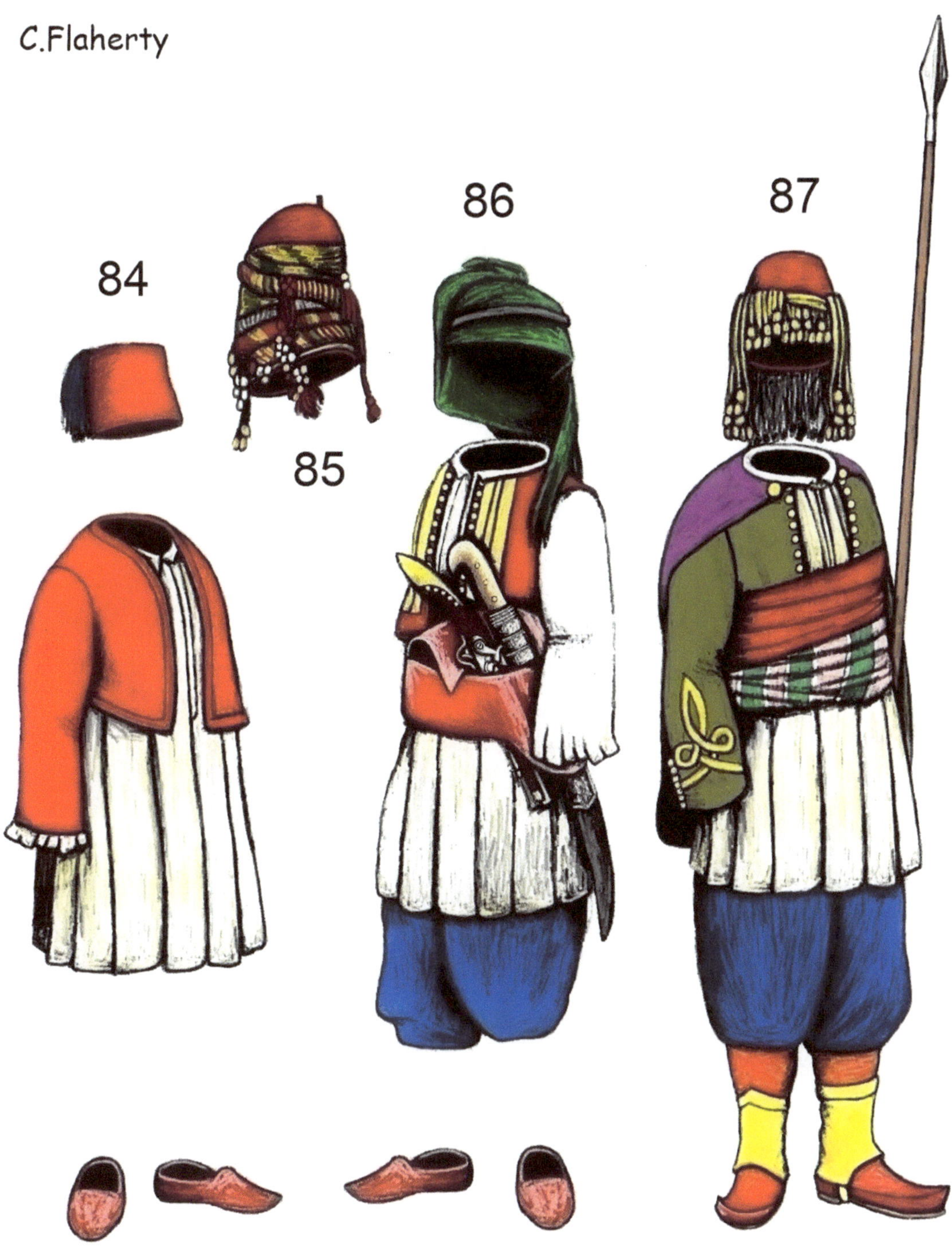

C.Flaherty
84
85
86
87

88
C.Flaherty

CHAPTER 10: NAVY

INTRODUCTION

By 1877, official strength of the Navy personnel was: 1,921 Navy Officers of all ranks, and 11,500 Navy Soldiers (Sailors), and 3,500 Galeonjees: Navy (Marine) Infantry Soldiers[198]. The 1861 Era Navy changed dramatically from the Crimean War Period, where:

> "except for ineffectual naval bombardments and the transportation of troops, the … Navy remained a self-made prisoner in its own bases. This now changed, and the Navy benefited greatly from the Sultan's fascination with new technology. A completely new fleet of up-to-date ironclad cruisers and monitors were purchased from Britain and France."[199]

Sultan Abdulaziz inherited from his predecessor Sultan Abdulmecid, a fleet of warships that had been in the process of converting from sail to steam power. The fleet of Vapuru: Armed Steamship in the Crimean War Period consisted of the following vessels:

VAPURU: ARMED STEAMSHIP		
NAME	GUNS	CREW
Mecidiye	29	284
Ta'if [Taif]	29	284
Feyz-i-Bari [Faisi-Bari; Feyza-i-Bahri]	29	284
Sa'ik-i-Gadi [Saik-i-Said]	29	284
Muhbir-i-Surur [Muphir-i-Surur]	20	379
Eser-i-Cedid	11	158
Ta'ir-i-Bahri	6	82
Eregli	8	67
Mesir-i-Bahri	9	67
Eser-i-Hayr	2	59

The armament of the Vapuru: Armed Steamships were Ottoman 12-okka (an Ottoman mass-weight measurement): 32-pounder, and 9-okka: 24-pounders[200]. It is generally understood that at the start of Sultan Abdulaziz' reign some of the existing sail ships were further, "modernized … sent to Britain to be fitted with steam engines."[201]

From January 1864, a public campaign began publishing in the Ceride-i-Askeriye: the first official Turkish Army newspaper to be published. The first articles looked at, "the importance of ironclads and the naval modernization to be implemented by the Sultan."[202] The first issue of the Ceride-i-Askeriye reported new Officials were to be assigned to ships, and titled Hoca: Teacher, and were to be ranked as Officers organized into four new classes according to the type of ship, on which they served:

Navy Miralai: Colonel	Ship-of-the-Line
Navy Bimbashi: Major	Frigate
Navy Mulazim-i-Evvel: Full-Lieutenant	Corvette
Mulazim-i-Sani: Lieutenant	Brig

---

198 United States Government, 1877.
199 Uyar, 2009.
200 Bal, 2010.
201 Dal, 2015.
202 Dal, 2015.

The third issue of the Ceride-i-Askeriye (published 31 January 1864), stated that the Navy was to organize into three ship's functional classes: Sefain-i-Safiyye (Warships); Sefain-i-Muhafaza (Coastal Guard Ships); and, Sefain-i-Nakliye (Transport Vessels). The third issue of the January 1864 Ceride-i-Askeriye article also carried a proclamation from the Sultan,

> "Underlining the modernization of the warships, the Sultan expressed his view in the same article that the battleships available in the Navy were not equivalent with the developed condition of European navies, and therefore it was obligatory to abandon the building of wooden ships and to adopt the construction of ironclads."[203]

The new Naval policy committed the Ottoman State to a purchasing programme for ironclads from Europe, notably England and France, and creating a local technical infrastructure within the Ottoman Empire for building and maintaining ironclads[204]. By the end of the reign of Sultan Abdulaziz, the Navy (by 1875) had a total of 111 ships, consisting of: 27 (later reduced to 26) ironclads; and, some 85 wooden and other armour-plated vessels. However, in terms of the actual operational fleet, this number of ships was much less according to an 1877 United States Government Foreign Relations Turkish Navy report:

> "The official Navy-list represents a much greater force than is here represented, as the names of a number of old wooden hulks are still retained , and also those of a few steamers, which from the length of service they have seen are in anything but an efficient condition and of little use as either transports or fighting-craft."[205]

The remaining wooden fleet ships, were: five frigates; eleven corvettes; two gun vessels; and, eleven gunboats, seven of which were armour-plated. Four of the known operational frigates cruising in the Levant, were all steam ships, and these were the: Selimieh, of 50 guns, Ertogrul (50 guns), Hundevendeghair (50 guns), and the Nasul Aziz (50 guns)[206]. It is known that the Selimieh armament consisted of ten Krupp 24-pounders, and several 6-pounders[207]. According to the 1877 United States Turkish Navy report, the armament of these vessels consisted principally of smooth-bore cannons, 42-pounders, and some 68-pounders, "but on the upper deck they all carry very heavy revolving guns of the latest pattern."[208]

Recent historical research, identifies the 78 gun Ship-of-the-Line Peyk-i-Zafer, was converted in Britain in 1856 to a steam screw ship. In 1858, the Tersane-i-Amire: Imperial Arsenal launched the 68-gun screw Ships-of-the-Line Sadiye and Fethiye. Converted in Britain in 1864, was the 96 gun screw Ship-of-the-Line Kosova, along with the 50 gun Frigates Ertugrul, Hudavendigar and Nasr-ul Aziz. In 1870, the 52 gun screw Frigate Selimiye, was launched by the Tersane-i-Amire: Imperial Arsenal.

The 1877 United States Turkish Navy report identified ships (using old spellings) operating in various fleet duties:

(1) Steam powered screw Corvettes were named: Sinope, Edirneh, Mussafir, Lebnan, Mansour-ab, Broussa, Ismir, lskeuderia, Outarit, Meyziee, and the Zouave. The vessels carried some 12 or 14 small calibre smooth-bore guns, and a heavy rifled revolving gun on the forecastle.

(2) Two gun-vessels were used on the Red Sea. Called the: Sedkul Bahar and Beirut, they each carry four, or five guns, including one heavy and others a lighter calibre.

(3) Four steam gun-boats, called the Akya, Shefket, Snnneh, and Varna carried light guns.

203 Dal, 2015.
204 Dal, 2015.
205 United States Government, 1877.
206 United States Government, 1877.
207 Crawford, 2013.
208 United States Government, 1877.

▼ In 1860, the Navy had the following sailing ships in service (the ship's names are in old, or alternative spellings)[13]:

NAME	TYPE
Kosova	Ship-of-the-Line
Fethiye	Ship-of-the-Line
Sadiye	Ship-of-the-Line
Peyk-i-Zafer	Ship-of-the-Line
Mahmudiye	Ship-of-the-Line
Tesrifiye	Ship-of-the-Line
Mukaddeme-i-Hayr	Ship-of-the-Line
Serafettin	Frigate
Mesir-i-Ferah	Corvette
Burc-i-Seref	Corvette
Sinop	Corvette
Izmir	Corvette
Alayis-i-Derya	Corvette
Necat-i-Fer	Corvette
Fecr-i-Sefid	Brig
Kavi Zafer	Brig
Serefnuma	Brig
Feth-i-Huner	Brig
Ahter	Brig
Tab-i-Dar	Brig
Tir-i-Zafer	Brig
Ferahnuma	Brig

IRONCLADS

In 1864, the first Ottoman ironclads were ordered from Britain[209]. The ironclads fell into a number of design classes. Seven were the central battery types; another five, were the broadside type; two were barbette battery types; two were casemate types, two were coast defence turret ships, two were armoured rams; and seven, were river monitors. In 1867, the fleet numbered decreased by one vessel, when the Fatih was purchased by Prussia on 6 February 1867.

Central Battery Ironclads		7
Broadside Ironclads		5
Barbette Battery Ironclads		2
Casemate Ironclads		2
Coast Defence Turret Ship		2
Armoured Rams		2
River Monitors		7
TOTAL:		27

209 Yener, 2009.

Some 12 vessels were purchased from England, and 10 were built in France, and one was ordered from an Austrian shipbuilding company. More ships, were purchased from France by the Egyptian Governorship and transferred to the Turkish Navy on 29 August 1868. These were the: Necm-i-Sevket, and Asar-i-Sevket (both Central Battery types); Asar-i-Tevfik (Barbette Battery type); Hifzurrahman and Lutf-i-Celil (both Seagoing Monitors). By 1870, two Central Battery ironclads named the Nusretiye and Mukaddeme-i-Hayr, and two River Monitors, the Hizber and Seyfi had been constructed in the Imperial Naval Arsenal.

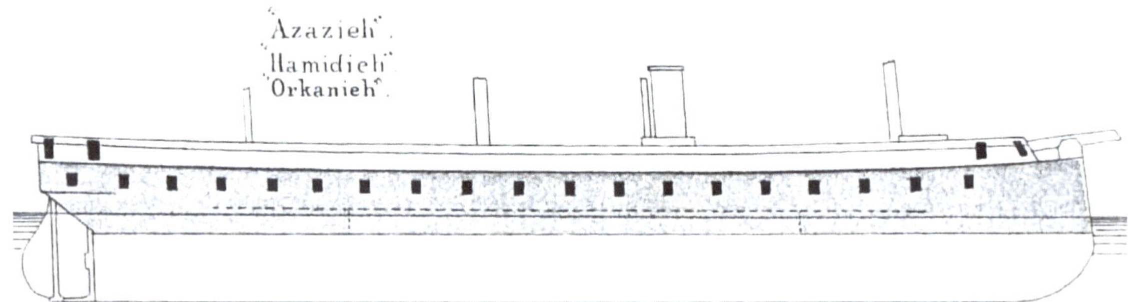

▲ Portside view of the design for three 1864 Ironclad Frigates Azazieh [Aziziye], Hamidieh [Osmaniye], and Orkanieh [Orhaniye]. These ships were Broadside-types, carrying 24 cannons and guns: fourteen 8-inch (150-pounder) Armstrong rifled muzzle-loading cannons; and, ten 40-pounder Armstrong rifled breech-loading guns. The vessels had a displacement of 6,400 tons, and crew of 640[210].

OCEAN-GOING IRONCLAD FLEET

The following set of tables shows the ironclads constructed for the Navy between 1864 and 1876:

LAUNCH DATE	CLASS & SHIP'S NAME	TYPE IRONCLAD	DISPLACEMENT (TONS)	GUNS	CREW
1864	Osmaniye	Broadside	6,400	24*	640
1864	Aziziye	Broadside	6,400	24*	640
1864	Orhaniye	Broadside	6,400	24*	640
1864	Mahmudiye	Broadside	6,400	25**	640

* Osmaniye Class armaments: fourteen 8-inch (150-pounder) Armstrong rifled muzzle-loading cannon; and, ten 40-pounder Armstrong rifled breech-loading guns.
** Mahmudiye armament: One 9-inch (250-pounder) Armstrong rifled muzzle-loading cannon; fourteen 8-inch (150-pounder) Armstrong rifled muzzle-loading cannon; and, ten 40-pounder Armstrong rifled breech-loading guns.

LAUNCH DATE	CLASS & SHIP'S NAME	TYPE IRONCLAD	DISPLACEMENT (TONS)	GUNS	CREW
1868	Asar-i-Sevket	Central Battery	2,080	5*	170
1868	Necm-i-Sevket	Central Battery	2,080	5*	170

* Asar-i-Sevket Class armaments: four 7-inch (110-pounder) Armstrong rifled breech-loading guns located in a central casemate; and, one 9-inch (250-pounder) Armstrong rifled muzzle-loading cannons, mounted in a revolving barbette atop the casemate.

---

210 Brassey, 1889.

LAUNCH DATE	CLASS & SHIP'S NAME	TYPE IRONCLAD	DISPLACEMENT	GUNS	CREW
1868	Asar-i-Tevfik	Barbette Battery	4,687	8*	320

* Asar-i-Tevfik armament: carried six 9-inch (250-pounder) Armstrong rifled muzzle-loading cannon; and two 200-pounders.

LAUNCH DATE	CLASS & SHIP'S NAME	TYPE IRONCLAD	DISPLACEMENT	GUNS	CREW
1868	Fatih-i Bulend	Broadside	2,762	4*	169

* Fatih-i-Bulend armament: carried four 9-inch (250-pounder) Armstrong rifled muzzle-loading cannons.

LAUNCH DATE	CLASS & SHIP'S NAME	TYPE IRONCLAD	DISPLACEMENT	GUNS	CREW
1868	Lutfu Celil [Lutf-i-Celil]	Seagoing Monitors	2,540	4*	122
1869	Hifz-ur Rahman [Hifzurrahman]	Seagoing Monitors	2,540	4*	122

* Luftu Celil [Lutf-i-Celil] Class armament: two 9-inch (250-pounder) Armstrong rifled muzzle-loading cannon mounted in a forward revolving turret; and, two 7-inch (110-pounder) Armstrong rifled breech-loading guns mounted in an aft revolving turret.

LAUNCH DATE	CLASS & SHIP'S NAME	TYPE IRONCLAD	DISPLACEMENT (TONS)	GUNS		CREW
1869	Avnillah	Casemate	2,080	4	9-inch guns	140
1869	Muin-i-Zafer	Casemate	2,080	4	9-inch guns	140
1870	Iclaliye	Barbette Battery	2,266	5*		180

* Iclaliye armament: two 9-inch (250-pounder) Armstrong rifled muzzle-loading cannon; and, three 7-inch (110-pounder) Armstrong rifled breech-loading guns.

1871	Nusretiye	Central Battery	6,594	NONE*	350

* The 6,600 ton ironclad Nusretiye (was later renamed the Hamidiye). Laid down in 1874, it was completed eleven years later, around 1882, and was totally obsolete.

LAUNCH DATE	CLASS & SHIP'S NAME	TYPE IRONCLAD	DISPLACEMENT (TONS)	GUNS		CREW
1870	Feth-i-Bulend	Central Battery	2,806	4	9-inch guns	169
1872	Mukaddeme-i-Hayr	Central Battery	2,806	4	9-inch guns	180
1874	Mesudiye	Central Battery	9,120	15*		700

* Mesudiye armament: twelve 10-inch (400-pounder) Armstrong rifled muzzle-loading cannon; and, three 7-inch (110-pounder) Armstrong rifled breech-loading guns.

1877-1878	Peyk-i-Seref	Armoured Ram	4,870	8*	250
1877-1878	Burc-i-Zafer	Armoured Ram	4,870	8*	250

* Peyk-i-Seref armament: four 12-inch (600-pounder) Armstrong rifled muzzle-loading cannon (25-ton gun); four 20-pounder Armstrong rifled breech-loaders. Armament included two torpedo carriages. Armed with Royal Navy's Whitehead 14-inch type; 18 knots (600 yards range); 26.5 pound warhead.

▲ The Payki Shereef [Peyk-i-Seref] Armoured Ram, in 1877[211].

DANUBE GUNBOAT FLOTILLA

The 1861 Era Danube Gunboat Flotilla underwent a considerable modernization with the purchase of five River Monitors in 1865 from France. These were the:

LAUNCH DATE	NAME	TYPE	DISPLACEMENT (TONS)	ARMSTRONG GUNS	CREW
1865	Feth-i-Islam	River Monitor	335	2*	45
1865	Semendire	River Monitor	335	2*	45
1865	Iskodra	River Monitor	335	2*	45
1865	Podgorice	River Monitor	335	2*	45
1865	Bogurtlen	River Monitor	335	2*	45

* Feth-i-Islam main armament: two Armstrong 64-pounder rifled muzzle-loading cannons. Another armament is also given for the Feth-i-Islam, and Semendire as two $4^5/_8$-inch Armstrong: 40-pounder rifled breech-loader[212]. While another, gives the armament types as two 32-pounder guns[213].

Later added to the Danube Gunboat Flotilla was two more River Monitors, built at the Tersane-i-Amire: Imperial Dockyards in Constantinople, in 1872, and 1873[214]. The new River Monitors were based on French designs that had two heavy guns mounted in a revolving turret[215]:

211 Wells, 1877.
212 Brassey, 2010.
213 Yener, 2009.
214 Branfill-Cook, 2016.
215 United States Government, 1877.

| 1872 | Hizber | River Monitor | 404 | 2* | 45 |
| 1873 | Seyfi | River Monitor | 404 | 2* | 45 |

* **Hizber and Seyfi turret armament: two 120-pounder muzzle-loading cannons[216]. Other references give the armament as two Krupp $4^{5}/_{8}$-inch cannons[217]. However, an 1877 United States Turkish Navy report lists these as two Krupp 80-pounders[218].**

An 1877 United States Turkish Navy report stated in relation to the Danube Gunboat Flotilla that its ships (using old spellings for the names), were stationed at the following locations, and named the commanders:

> "seven ironclad gunboats … were specially built for service on the Danube are named as follows: Fethi Islam (Moslem Victory), Bnyoordelan (Heart-piercer), Semandereh, Scodra, Podgoritza, Isber (Lion), and Saffeh (Sword). These craft … are armed with two light Armstrong guns … The first five on the list are already in the Danube, stationed at Widdin, and placed under the command of Kiritlee Hussein Pasha, an active officer of the Imperial Navy. The other two were launched but a short time ago at the arsenal up the Golden Horn, and are of a much improved type. They are each fitted with a revolving turret, in which are mounted two Krupp guns, 80-pounders"[219].

NAVY FLAGS

The 1861 Era Navy flew the Ottoman Government National Flag. Another flag used was the Pavillon de Marine: Navy Flag, which consisted of a red field with a centred white rectangular box. The Flamme de Guerre: Navy War Mast Pennant, was a long red streamer.

▲ The Ottoman Government National Flag in the 1861 Era, with a multi pointed star. Other variations had six, or five pointed stars.

---

216 Olender, 2017.
217 Brassey, 2010.
218 United States Government, 1877.
219 United States Government, 1877.

NAVY OFFICER'S UNIFORM AND RANK SYSTEM

The 1861 Era Navy Officer's frock coat was dark blue, double breasted, and it reached down to the knees[220]. It had a fall-down collar, and lapels that were closed by four pairs of large gilt metal buttons. A fifth (top pair) was visible between the lapels. A white shirt and collar was worn with a black bowtie cravat. Plain dark blue pants, and black shoes complete the dress. The Navy Officer's buckle was a cast brass circular type with open-framed keepers on either side of an olive, and laurel leaves wreath. Displayed inside the wreath, the Navy Crest pattern had two five-point stars on either side of an anchor, with an upwards pointing crescent over this. This was also the coat button design. Large gold fringed epaulettes, with gold tape bridles were worn. After 1853, and throughout the Crimean War Period, the Navy Officer (following the Army) used rank identifying epaulettes for three broad categories:

Senior Officer	Large gold rigid fringed epaulettes
Mid-Level Officer	Loose fringed gold epaulettes
Lower-Grade Officer	Fringeless gold epaulettes

After 1861, the new Navy Senior Officer's rank system consisted of wide, and narrow gold tape cuff-rings, with the top ring ending in a diamond-ended trefoil knot. The 1861 rank insignia for the Mushir: Admiral of the Fleet, was still in use in 1908[221], while the cuff rank insignia for a Navy Miralai: Colonel (Admiral), from 1861 is also known[222]. Remaining Navy Senior Officer's rank insignia likely used:

Navy Mousheer [Mushir]: Marshal (Grand Admiral)	One wide cuff ring, and two narrow rings, the top one ending in a diamond-ended trefoil knot
Navy Feriq [Ferik]: General de Division (Vice Admiral)	One wide cuff ring, and two narrow rings, the top ring one ending in a diamond knot
Navy Mir-el-Liwa [Liwa]: General de Brigade (Rear Admiral)	One wide cuff ring, and top narrow ring ending in a diamond knot
Navy Miralai: Colonel (Admiral)	Four cuff rings, with top one ending in a diamond knot

After 1861, the new Navy Officer's rank system consisted of gold tape cuff-rings, with the top ring ending in a diamond knot:

Navy Bimbashi: Major	Three cuff rings, top one ending in a diamond knot
Navy Yuzbashi: Captain	Two cuff rings, top one ending in a diamond knot
Navy Mulazim-i-Evvel: Full-Lieutenant	One cuff ring ending in a diamond knot

1861 PETTY OFFICERS AND MIDSHIPMAN

The early Navy operated on a rank structure that was identical to that used in the Army. From 1861, onwards, this situation began to change as a result of new steam and ironclad technology being introduced requiring new branches of service, and technical ranks to be created following the practice in other Navies in the Period. Navy ranks for Junior Officers for the first time began to expand to include Petty Officers (ranked commonly as Warrant Officers), and Midshipman (the lowest rank of Navy Officer), than seen previously in the Crimean War, or earlier times. By 1876, however the situation changed again, and new levels of Junior Officers were created.

New Junior Officers, expanded from the pre-1853 Period, and given a new formal uniform consisting of an updated version of the basic lapel collared short blue jacket adopted by the Navy in the 1850s. This was a double buttoned sided waist jacket (open at the front), and closed with two chain linked buttons. It had a fall-down collar ending with broad lapels. Sleeves had deep round

220 Sevket, 1907.
221 Askeri Muze, 1986.
222 Basimevi, 1997.

folded-up cuffs, displaying three large tunic buttons. Petty Officers, and Midshipman wore Fez, however the Greek hat has been depicted[223]. Around the neck a broad black cravat was worn. A collarless pull-over shirt was tucked into white pants with a red broad waist band. Black shoes completed the outfit.

There is a depiction of an 1861 Era Navy Soldier wearing a particular hat described usually as, "Dortkose Fesli Bahriye Neferi: Navy Soldier with Square Fez"[224]. The Greek hat is somewhat similar to the Tirailleurs Algeriens Fez in the French Army of North Africa, it was a wide bellowing red wool felt Fez that was wider at the top, than its base, and like the Fez had a long tassel hanging from a cord. Traditionally, the Navy was the sole military institution to allow Christian Greek Sailors, and they distinctively wore a red wide domed bonnet[225][226]. It appears, in the 1861 Era Navy, there was still a distinction being made between Christian and Muslim Soldiers through their headgear.

The 1856 Islahat Fermani [Hatt-i Humayun]: Imperial Decree allowed for all Ottoman Empire citizens to serve in the military regardless of faith. It is generally known,

▲ Navy Button pattern for 1861. The Navy Crest pattern displayed two five-point stars on either side of an anchor, with an upwards pointing crescent over this. Used till 1903, when a version was introduced with three, six (or five) pointed stars over an anchor. Represented three seas the Ottoman Empire had traditional claim over: Black, Aegean and Mediterranean seas. After 1903, the crest was changed to an anchor over an upwards pointing crescent.

"[with] … disappearance of the Cossack Cavalry Regiment … [around 1876] … [and] … Christian Albanian mercenaries, and Greek Sailors from the ranks of the Army and Navy, by the 1870s the Ottoman military consisted of only Muslim rank and file"[227].

The 1861 Era Navy Soldier wearing a Greek hat, indicating he was a Christian Greek Sailor is likely to have been a pre-1870s practice. Disappearing by the end of the reign of Sultan Abdulaziz.

1861 JUNIOR OFFICERS

1861 Era Junior Officers received a new type of blue collared pull-over shirt, which had a short vent closure, with a standing collar (that may have folded-down over the Soldier's shoulders) that had a thick red cord, running around the base tied into a large bowtie. Sleeves had folded-up square-ended cuffs. The pull-over shirt was tucked into white pants with a red broad waist band. Black shoes completed the outfit.

Illustrations of the 1861 Era Junior Officers' uniform shows the collar and cuffs decorated with three lines of red tape. The ranks of Navy Onbasi: Corporal, Cavus: Sergeant, Bascavus: Sergeant-Major, in this Era corresponded directly to their Army counterparts. It is assumed the rank system was displayed on the collar and cuffs:

One line of cuff and collar tape:	Onbasi: Corporal
Two lines of cuff and collar tape:	Cavus: Sergeant
Three lines of cuff and collar tape:	Bascavus: Sergeant-Major

---

223 Basimevi, 1997.
224 Basimevi, 1997.
225 Sevket, 1907.
226 Basimevi, 1997.
227 Uyar, 2009.

By 1876, the situation changed again, and several new levels of Junior Officers were created, more commonly associated with conventional Navy establishments, where Sailor's trade, were in effect their rank, and new trade-ranks, such as those seen in the Royal Navy: Ordinary Stoker, Stoker, Leading Stoker, Stoker Petty Officer and Chief Stoker, began to appear in the Navy as well.

1861 NAVY SOLDIERS UNIFORM

An 1907 dated set of illustration show the basic Navy Soldier's uniform, as a plain blue shirt that button along the right shoulder[228][229]. In colder weather, they had short blue jackets with plain cuffs[230][231]. Around the neck a broad black cravat was worn on dress occasions. Navy Soldiers wore the pullover shirt tucked into white pants with a broad red waist band. Black shoes completed the outfit. On board the ship a Navy Soldier went bare footed traditionally (the practice continued into WW1).

1861 GALEONJEES: NAVY (MARINE) INFANTRY SOLDIERS

The 1861 Era Galeonjees: Navy (Marine) Infantry Soldiers, had expanded in numbers greatly from their Crimean War organization, and now numbered some 3,500 Soldiers[232]. Converted to wear Zouave uniforms, that were nearly identical to the Line Infantry version. However, it did not have any piping running along the top of the sleeve shoulder. This is according to an illustration appearing in an Early 20th Century Turkish set of Navy uniforms[233]. The only other distinguishing feature was use of a buckle-plate with an upwards pointing crescent and an anchor between the crescent horns. The buckle was known in later periods, and appears to be indicated in a later illustration[234]. It is also possible that the 1861 version displayed a badge consisting of an upwards pointing crescent over an anchor – following the design of the Navy Officer's buckle used at the time.

FIGURE 89: Navy Captain.

FIGURE 90: Navy Mousheer [Mushir]: Marshal's rank cuff details.

FIGURE 91: Navy Officer's buckle.

FIGURE 92: Navy Bimbashi: Major's rank cuff details.

FIGURE 92a: Navy Yuzbashi: Captain's rank cuff details.

FIGURE 92b: Navy Mulazim-i-Evvel: Full-Lieutenant's rank cuff details.

FIGURE 93: Flamme de Guerre: Navy War Mast Pennant.

FIGURE 94: Pavillon de Marine: Navy Flag.

FIGURE 95: Ordinary Navy Soldier.

FIGURE 96: Petty Officer wearing a Greek hat.

FIGURE 97: Navy Bascavus: Sergeant-Major.

FIGURE 97a: Navy Infantry Cavus: Sergeant.

FIGURE 97b: Navy Onbasi: Corporal.

FIGURE 98: Navy Infantry buckle.

FIGURE 99: Ottoman National Flag with multipoint star.

FIGURE 100: Navy Infantry.

FIGURE 101: Navy Infantry Onbasi: Corporal.

FIGURE 102: Navy Infantry Cavus: Sergeant.

FIGURE 103: Navy Infantry Bascavus: Sergeant-Major.

228 Sevket, 1907.
229 Basimevi, 1997.
230 Sevket, 1907.
231 Basimevi, 1997.
232 United States Government, 1877.
233 Basimevi, 1997.
234 Basimevi, 1997.

C.Flaherty

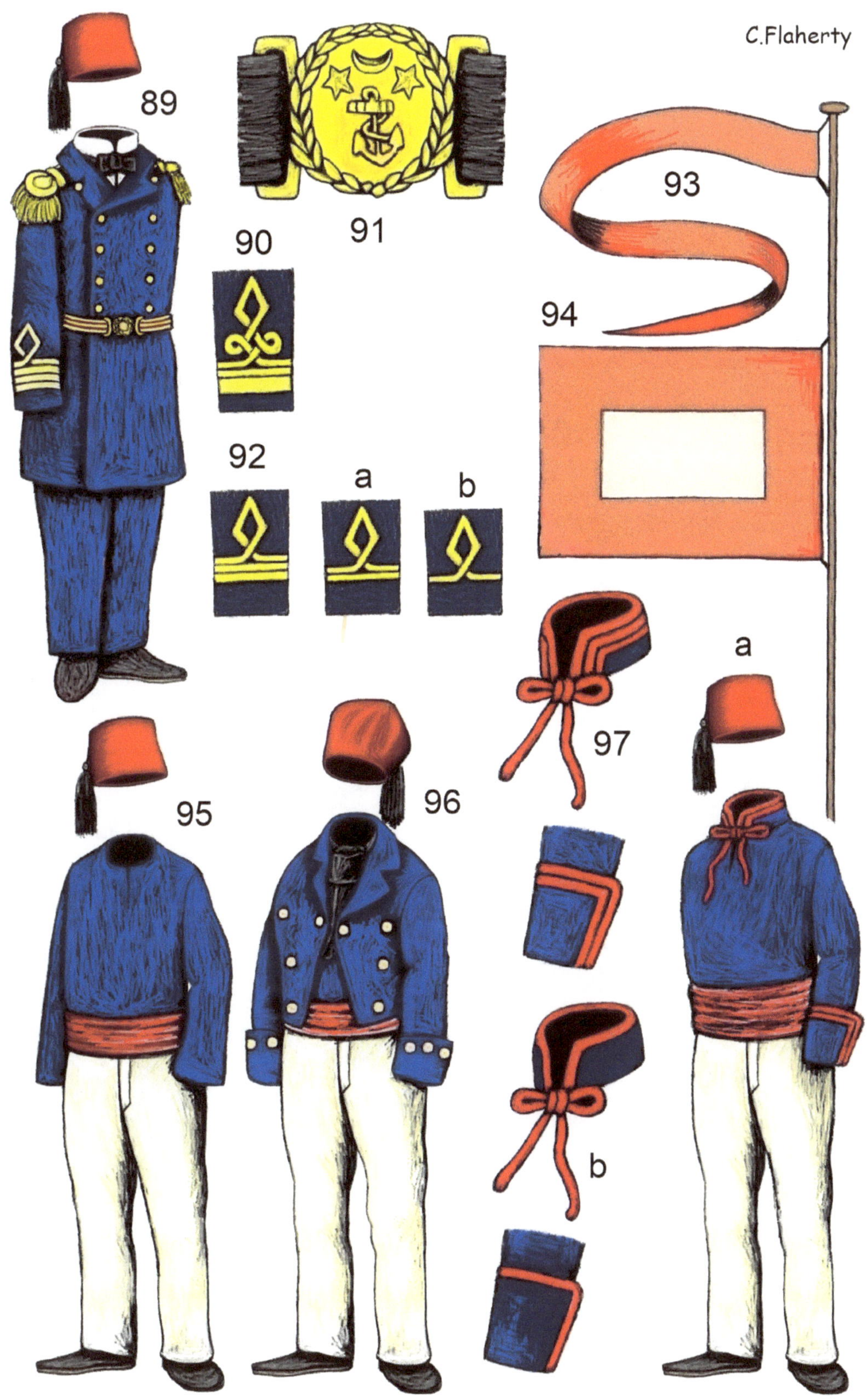

89
91
90
93
94
92
a
b
95
96
97
a
b
81

C.Flaherty

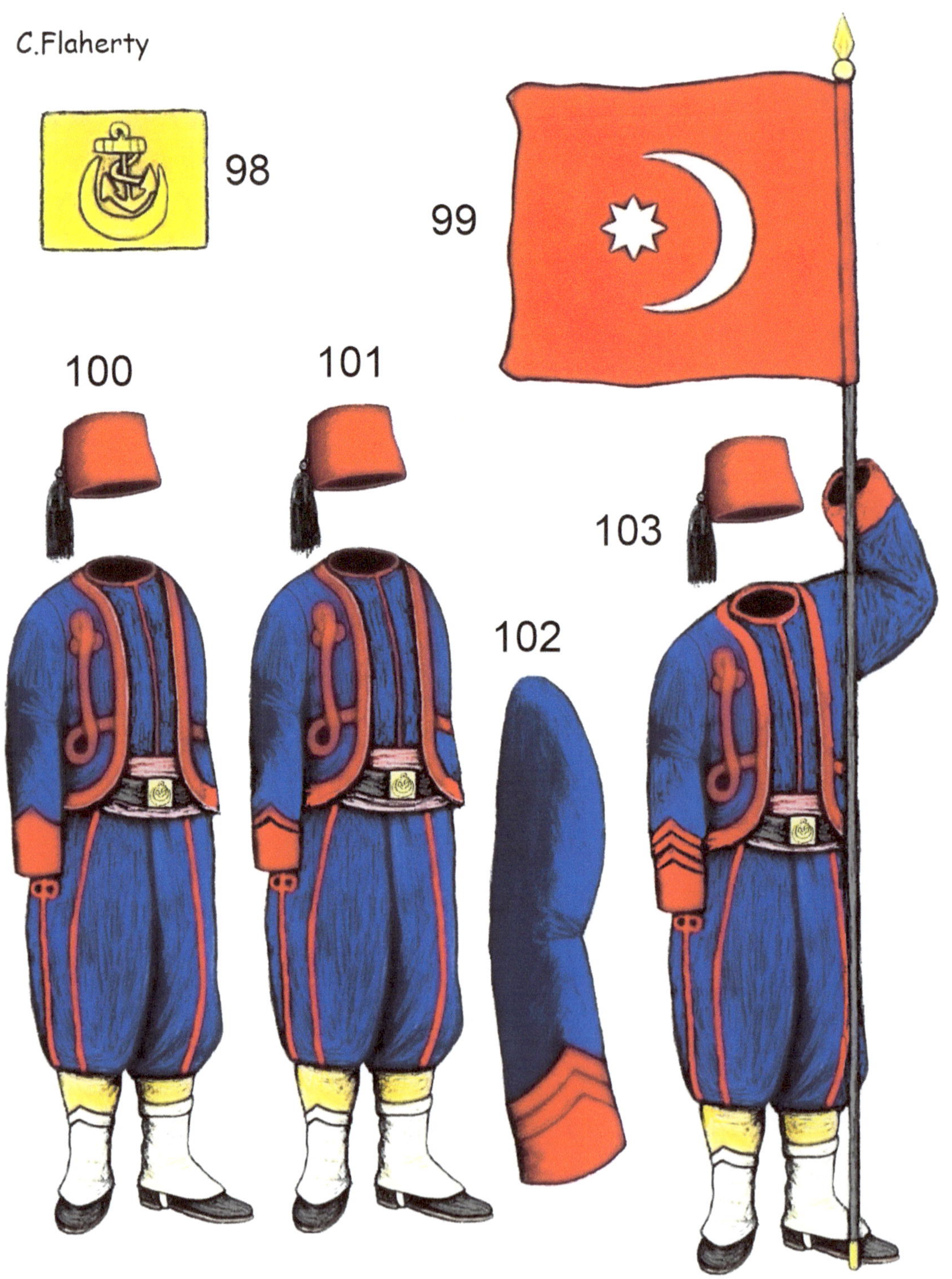

98

99

100

101

102

103

REFERENCES

- Anatole, A. Bocquin, J-A. 1895 Pasha (General). Lemercier et Cie. Anne S.K. Brown Military Collection. BDR: 382689.
- Aksan, V.H. 2013 Mobilization of Warrior Populations in the Ottoman Context, 1750-1850. Zurcher, E-J. (Editor) Fighting for a Living: A Comparative Study of Military Labour 1500-2000. Amsterdam University Press.
- Askeri Muze [National Army Military Museum, Istanbul]. 2017 Harbiye Askeri Muzesi Uniforma Katalogu [Military Museum Uniform Catalogue]. Askeri Muze ve Kultur Sitesti Komutanligi Yayinlari.
- Askeri Muze [National Army Military Museum, Istanbul]. 1986 Osmanli Askeri Teskilat ve Kiyafetleri [Ottoman Military Organization and Uniforms]: 1876-1908. Askeri Muze ve Kultur Sitesti Komutanligi Yayinlari.
- Badem, C. 2010 The Ottoman Crimean War (1853-1856). Brill.
- Bal, N. 2010 Ottoman Shipbuilding Technology: The Period of Steam Ships. Master's Dissertation. Mimar Sinan Fine Arts University.
- Basimevi, K. 1997 Tarihten Punumuze Deniz Kuvvetleri Personel Kiyafetlerinin Gecirdigi Asamalar [Ottoman Turkish Navy Organization and Uniforms from 1363 till 1989]. Dz.K.K. Ligi Karargah Basimevi: Ankara.
- Bennett, J. 2018 The Aynali Martini: the Ottoman Army's First Modern Rifle. Anatolica. Volume XLIV.
- Blackwood, W. 1841 Blackwood's Edinburgh Magazine. Volume 50.
- Boisselier, H. 1931 [-1951]. 7er Bon. de Zouaves 1834: Tambour and Lieutenant. Unbound Portfolio. Paris. Anne S.K. Brown Military Collection. BDR: 250708.
- Boisselier, H. 1931 [-1951] Chasseurs d'Afrique 1832: Officier et Soldat, C. des Indigenes. Unbound Portfolio. Paris. Anne S.K. Brown Military Collection. BDR: 250698.
- Boisselier, H. 1959 Musicians, 1811. Painting.
- Boussod, J. 1897 Les Bachi-Bouzouks. Souvenirs de Crimee. Manzi, Joyant & Co.
- Brassey, T. 2010 The British Navy: Its Strength, Resources, and Administration. Cambridge University Press.
- Brassey, T. 1889 The Naval Annual 1888-9. Portsmouth: J. Griffin and Co.
- Branfill-Cook, R. 2016 River Gunboats: An Illustrated Encyclopaedia. Casemate Publishers.
- Breville [de], J.O. 'JOB' 1898 Officier de Zouaves en Costume Orient (1830-1834). L'Epopee du Costume Militaire Francais; Aquarelles et Dessins Originaux De Job [French Military Uniforms]. Societe Francaise d'Editons d'Art.
- Brindesi, J. Bettannier, J. (Lithographer) 1855 Nizami Djedid Bimbachi, Chef de Bataillon la 1re. Reforme du Sultan Mahmoud. Anciens Costumes Turcs de Constantinople. Paris: Lemercier. York Public Library [The]. Collection: Image ID: 85574.
- Bulyovszky, K. 1873 Fegyvertan [Armament]. Budapest.
- Cetin, M. Kok, R. 2016 Kirim Savasi Sirasinda Osmanli Devleti ile Muttefik Devletler Arasindaki Silah Ticareti [The Arms Trade Between the Ottoman Empire and the Allies During the Crimean War] (1854-1856). History Studies International Journal of History (December).
- Charles, V. 1860 Zouave de la Ligne (Tenue de Guerre). Vinkhuijzen, H.J. [Collection]. New York Public Library [The]. Image ID: 830409.
- Chivers, C.J. 2013 The Gun: The Story of the AK-47. Penguin.
- Cliff, D. 1997 Polish Volunteers with the Turkish Army. The War Correspondent. Volume 14. Number 4 (January).
- Cox, M. Lenton, J. 1997 Crimean War Basics: Organisation and Uniforms: Russia and Turkey. Partizan Press.
- Crawford, K.R. Mitiukov, N.W. 2013 Identification of the Parameters of Naval Artillery. Prague: Vedecko Vydavatelske Centrum.
- Czajkowski, C [Mehmed Sadyk Pasha, Pasza]. 1962 Moje Wspomnienia o Wojnie 1854 Roku. Warsaw: Wydawnicstwo Ministerstwa Obrony Narodowej [My Memories of the War of 1854. Warsaw: Publishing House of the Ministry of National Defense]. Private Translation.

- Czajkowski, M. [Sadyk Pasha] 1883 [-1904] Turkish Anecdotes. Moscow: Journal of Russkaya Starina.
- Dal, D. 2015 The Modernization of the Ottoman Navy During the Reign of Sultan Abdulaziz (1861-1876). PhD Thesis. The University of Birmingham.
- Demoulin, V. Chartier, H. 1897 [-1904]. Turquie (Armes, Drapeaux, Armee). Nouveau Larousse Illustre [New Larousse Illustrated French Language Encyclopedia].
- Deroy, I. 1855 Debarquement de l'Armee Turque e Eupatoria: Commandee par Omer Pasha. Illustration. Anne S.K. Brown Military Collection. BDR: 233574.
- Dodd, G. 1856 Pictorial History of the Russian War, 1854-56. Edinburgh and London: W.R. Chambers.
- Drury, I. 2012 The Russo-Turkish War 1877. Osprey Publishing.
- Druck [der], K.K. 1905 Die Turkische Armee. Druck der K.K. Hof- und Staatsdruckerei. Wien.
- Ducel, G. 1860 Mameluck, 1813-1815 [Mameluke of the Guard]. Photograph. Anne S.K. Brown Military Collection. BDR: 235795.
- Dunn, J.P. 2013 Khedive Ismail's Army. Taylor & Francis Ltd.
- Encyclopædia Britannica. 2022 Bashi-Bazouk. Ottoman Soldier. Website.
- Eruretin, M. 2001 Osmanli Madalyalari Ve Nisanlari [Ottoman Medals and Orders: Documented History]. DMC.
- Esposito, G. 2017 Armies of the Italian Wars of Unification 1848–70 (1): Piedmont and the Two Sicilies. Osprey Publishing.
- Garnier, V. 1856 Piemontes in Crimea. Print Album. Maggi. G.B. Torino.
- Gerome, J-L. 1869 Bashi-Bazouks. Metropolitan Museum of Art. Collection. Object ID: 440723.
- Hacisalihoglu, M. 2007 Standard Presentation to Newly Founded Regiment, in 1844 by Sultan Abdulmecid. Illustration. Osmanli Imparatorlugu'nda Zorunlu Askerlik Sistemine Gecis Ordu-millet Dusuncesi [The Transition to Compulsory Military Service in the Ottoman Empire]. Toplumsal Tarih, Number 164 (August).
- Illustrated London News [The]. 1876 Barracks of the Bashi-Bazouks at the Chibouk Chular Khan, Adrianople [Edirne]. The New York Public Library Digital Collections. Illustration. Image ID831284.
- Imperial Dockyards. 1861 [-1876] Ship's Aftercastle Coat of Arms Decoration with Tugra on a Shield for Sultan Abdulaziz. Tersane-i-Amire [Imperial Arsenal], Constantinople.
- Karakoc, E. Mete, A.S. 2020 Osmanli Askeri Modernizasyon Calismalari Cercevesinde Yapilan Silah Alimlarinin Mali Yapiya Etkileri [The Effects of Firearm Purchasing on the Ottoman Financial Structure During the Military Modernization]: 1853-1908. SUTAD. Volume 49 (August).
- Koppen, F [Von]. Gleichen, E. Richard Knotel, R. (Illustrator) 1890 The Armies of Europe Illustrated. London: William Clowes & Sons, Limited.
- Lovell, M.S. 1998 A Rage to Live. Hachette, UK.
- Mallett, H.H. 2013 Fighting Peacocks: The Colourful History of Zouaves. Military History Now (May).
- Mango, A. 1999 Ataturk. John Murray.
- Mansel, P. 2005 Dressed to Rule: Royal and Court Costume from Louis XIV to Elizabeth II. Yale University Press.
- Money, E. 1857 Twelve Months with the Bashi-Bazouks. London: Chapman and Hall.
- Murray, N. 2013 The Rocky Road to the Great War: The Evolution of Trench Warfare to 1914. Potomac Books, Inc.
- Norman, C.A. 1985 Turkish Uniforms of the Crimean Era. Soldiers of the Queen (Magazine of The Victorian Military Society). Issue Number 85.
- Olender, P. 2017 Russo-Turkish Naval War 1877-1878. MMP Books.
- Ollier, E. 1890 Illustrated History of the Russo-Turkish War. Volume I. London.
- Pawly, R. 2012 Napoleon's Mamelukes. Osprey Publishing.
- Preziosi, A [Count]. 1857 Illustration of Albanians Mercenaries in the Ottoman Army. Published by Lemercier & Cie, Paris.
- Radcliffe, J.N. 1858 The Hygiene of the Turkish Army. Report with Additions, from the Sanitary Review. John Churchill, New Burlington Street, London.
- Raffet, A. 1854 Armee Turque: Artillerie-a-Pied; Chasseur; Infanterie de Ligne (Sergent); and, Bachi-Bouzoug. Illustration. Anne S.K. Brown Military Collection. BDR: 226574.

- Rice, E. 2001 Captain Sir Richard Francis Burton: A Biography. Da Capo Press.
- Rigo, J.A.V. 1840 Kabyle: Berber of Algeria or Tunisia. Lebref et Cie. Vinkhuijzen, H.J. [Collection]. New York Public Library [The]. Image ID: 826678.
- Robinson, R. 1988 The Crimean War: Parts 1 to 4. Miniature Wargames (Magazine).
- Roubicek, M. 1978 Modern Ottoman Troops, 1797-1915: In Contemporary Pictures. Franciscan Printing Press.
- Ruhl, M. 1900 [Circa: Published From] Die Armeen der Balkan-Staaten. II. Turkei u. Griechenland [The Armies of the Balkans. Turkey and Greece: Volume 2]. Leipzig: Moritz Ruhl.
- Sakul, K. 2011 General Observations on the Ottoman Military Industry, 1774-1839. Gonergun, F. Raina, D. (Editors) Problems of Organization and Standardization Europe and Asia: Historical Studies on the Transmission, Adoption and Adaptation of Knowledge. Springer.
- Sevket, M. [Mahmoud Chevket Pasha] 1907 L'Organization et les Uniformes de l'Armee Ottomanne. Premiere Partie.
- Shaw, S.J. Shaw, E.K. 1977 History of the Ottoman Empire and Modern Turkey; Reform, Revolution, and Republic: The Rise of Modern Turkey 1808-1975 (Volume 2). Cambridge University Press.
- Slade, A. 1867 Turkey and the Crimean War: A Narrative of Historical Events. London: Smith, Elder & Co.
- Turker, G.K. 2022 Osmanli Imparatorlgu Askeri Kiyafetleri [Military Clothing of the Ottoman Empire] 1826-1922. Hisart Canli Tarih Muzeesi Kultur Yayinian 2.
- United States Government. 1877 United States Congressional Serial Set. Volume 1741. U.S. Government Printing Office.
- Unknown. Late-19th Century. 2nd Regiment of Polish Sultan Cossacks. Illustration.
- Unknown. 1820 [-1898; Handwritten Attribution: 1859] Egypt. Albanian Infantry Regiment. Vinkhuijzen, H.J. [Collection]. New York Public Library [The]. Image ID: 1606991.
- Unknown. 1843 Infanterist der Regulaizen Truppen Abd'el Kada. Vinkhuijzen, H.J. [Collection]. New York Public Library [The]. Image ID: 438529.
- Unknown. 1847 Soldat der Regularen Infanterie Abdel-Kaders Aus Algier. Lithography. Brussel-Leipzig. York Public Library [The]. Collection: Image ID: 826691.
- Unknown. 1850 [-1896] Imam du Regiment. Vinkhuijzen, H.J. [Collection]. New York Public Library [The]. Image ID: 435723.
- Unknown. 1850 [-1896; Handwritten Attribution: 1885] Garde du Palais. Turkey. Vinkhuijzen, H.J. [Collection]. New York Public Library [The]. Image ID: 435690.
- Unknown. 1850 [-1896; Handwritten Attribution: 1885] Infanterie. Turkey. Vinkhuijzen, H.J. [Collection]. New York Public Library [The]. Image ID: 435692.
- Unknown. 1850 [-1896; Handwritten Attribution: 1885] Infanterie (Garde). Turkey. Vinkhuijzen, H.J. [Collection]. New York Public Library [The]. Image ID: 435691.
- Unknown. 1850 [-1896; Handwritten Attribution: 1885] Set of Turkish Court Uniforms Identifying Chef des Bachi-Boszouks, Chef des Gardes du Palais, and General de Division. Vinkhuijzen, H.J. [Collection]. New York Public Library [The]. Image ID: 435696.
- Unknown. 1850 [-1896; Handwritten Attribution: 1885] Turkish Set of Court Uniforms Identifying Officier de Bachi-Bouzouks. Vinkhuijzen, H.J. [Collection]. New York Public Library [The]. Image ID: 435695.
- Unknown. 1854 Zouaves. Painting. Anne S.K. Brown Military Collection. BDR: 225021.
- Unknown. 1861 [Circa] Sultan Abdulaziz Sitting in His Turkish Army Dress Uniform. Carte de Visite.
- Unknown. 1876 Turkish Troops From a Sketch by Our Special Artist at Constantinople. The Graphic (1 July).
- Unknown. 1896 [-1909] Turkey. Turkische Cavallerie Tscherkessen. Vinkhuijzen, H.J. [Collection]. New York Public Library [The]. Image ID: 435767.
- Unknown. 1896 [-1909] Turkey. No Title Given: Another Version of the Mounted Turkische Cavallerie Tscherkessen. Vinkhuijzen, H.J. [Collection]. New York Public Library [The]. Image ID: 435748.
- Unknown. 1896 [-1909; Signature and 1887 Date] Turkische Truppen. Vinkhuijzen, H.J. [Collection]. New York Public Library [The]. Image ID: 435737.
- Unknown. 1896 [-1909] Turkey. Infantry of the Line, Private and Officer, Review Order. Vinkhuijzen,

H.J. [Collection]. New York Public Library [The]. Image ID: 435730.

- Unknown. 1896 [-1909] Turkey. Flag Officer and Accompanying Soldiers from the 1st Albanian Regiment of the Imperial Guard. Vinkhuijzen, H.J. [Collection]. New York Public Library [The]. Image ID: 435751.
- Unknown. 1896 [-1909] Turkey. Zeibek Infantry. Vinkhuijzen, H.J. [Collection]. New York Public Library [The]. Image ID: 435749.
- Urquhart, D. 1852 [-1869] The Ottoman Empire Under Abdul Medjid: The Military Strength of Turkey. London: Effingham Wilson, Royal Exchange.
- Uyar, M. Erickson, E.J. 2009 A Military History of the Ottomans: From Osman to Ataturk. Praeger.
- Vernet, H. 1860 Painting of a Bashi-Bazouks. Wallace Collection: Museum Number P593.
- Walsh, T. 1803 Journal of the Late Campaign in Egypt. Cadell & Davies, Strand, London.
- War Department. 1856 Army Clothing – Return to an Address of the Honourable. The House of Commons (11 August).
- War Office [The]. 2008 [The] 1915 Notes on the Turkish Army: With a Short Vocabulary of Turkish Words and Phrases. N & M Press.
- Wells, J.R. 1877 The New Turkish Ironclad Payki Shereef. The Illustrated London News. Number 2004. Volume 71 (8 December).
- Yener, E. 2009 Iron Ships and Iron Men: Naval Modernization in the Ottoman Empire, Russia, China and Japan from a Comparative Perspective 1830-1905. Thesis. Bogazici University.
- Yildiz, G. 2012 Ottoman Military Organization (1800-1918). Martel, G. (Editor) The Encyclopedia of War. Blackwell Publishing Ltd.
- Yorulmaz, N. 2014 Arming the Sultan: German Arms Trade and Personal Diplomacy in the Ottoman Empire Before World War I. Bloomsbury Publishing.
- Zengin, E. 2015 Tophane-i-Amire'den Imalat-i-Harbiye'ye Osmanli Devleti'nde Harp Sanayii [War Industry in the Ottoman Empire from Tophane-i-Amire to Manufacturing in the Harbiye] (1861-1923). Ph.D. Dissertation. Ataturk University.
- Zher, E. Barbant. (Engraver) 1885 Types and Costumes. Group of Zeibek. Reclus, E. Ravenstein, E.G. (Editor) The Universal Geography, the Earth and its inhabitants. Virtue & Co Ltd, London.

OTHER TITLES ABOUT THE WORLD ARMIES IN XIX C.

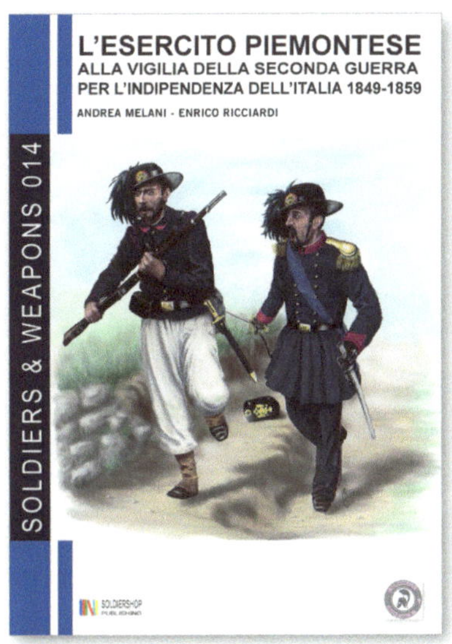

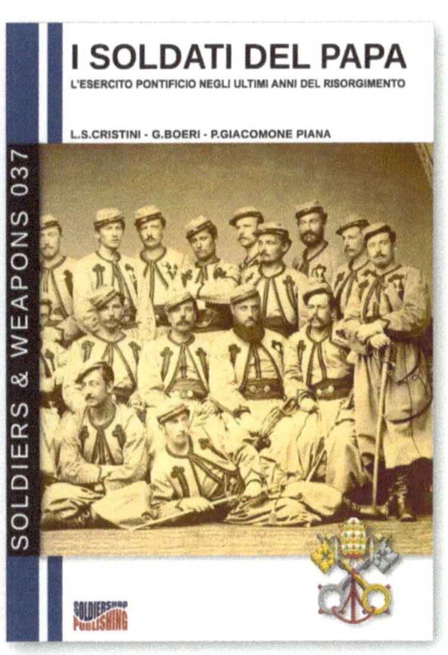

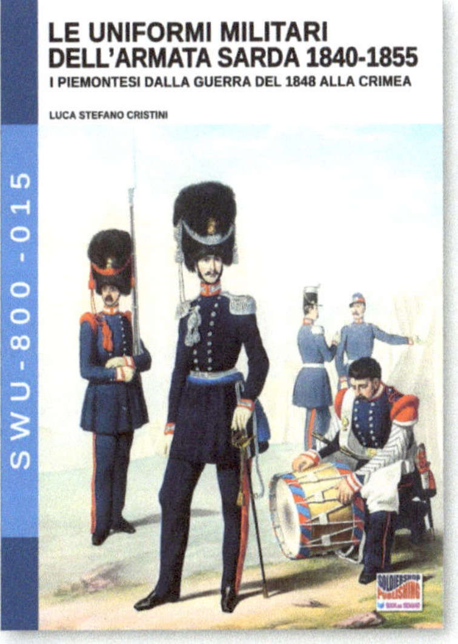

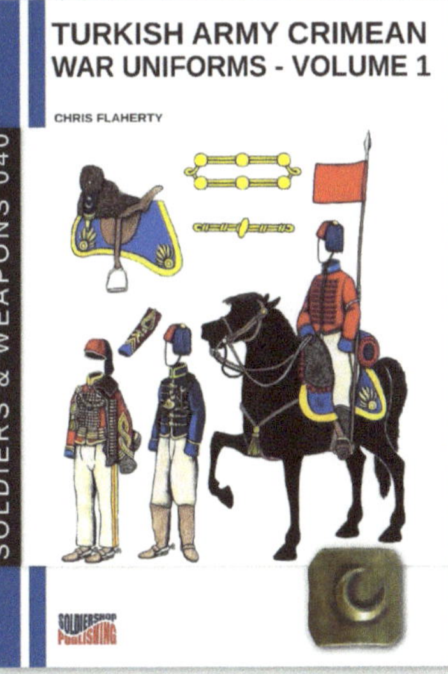

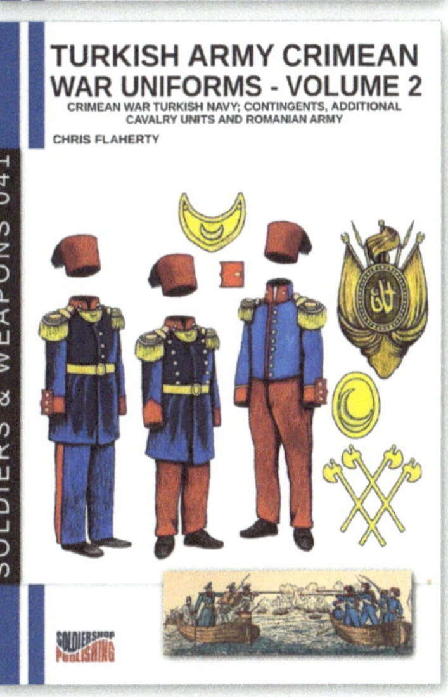

SOLDIERS&WEAPONS 042